girl time

Other books by Laura Jensen Walker

Thanks for the Mammogram!
Mentalpause
Dated Jekyll, Married Hyde
Love Handles for the Romantically Impaired
God Rest Ye Grumpy Scroogeymen, with Michael Walker

girl time

a celebration of chick flicks, bad hair days & good friends

laura jensen walker

Fleming H. Revell
A Division of Baker Book House Co
Grand Rapids, Michigan 49516

Published by Fleming H. Revell
a division of Baker Book House Company
P.O. Box 6287, Grand Rapids, MI 49516-6287
www.bakerbooks.com

Printed in the United States of America

Published in association with the literary agency of Alive Communications, Inc., 7680 Goddard Street, Suite 200, Colorado Springs, CO 80920.

Library of Congress Cataloging-in-Publication Data
Walker, Laura Jensen.
    Girl time : a celebration of chick flicks, bad hair days, and good friends / Laura Jensen Walker.
        p.   cm.
    ISBN 0-8007-5894-3 (pbk.)
    1. Christian women—Religious life. 2. Female friendship—Religious aspects—Christianity. I. Title.
BV4527.W335 2004
248.8'43—dc22   2003019125

For (in alphabetical order) Annette, Jan, Katie, Lana,
Lisa, Lonnie, Mom, Pat, and Sheri
with love and gratitude for your friendship

and for all my other girlfriends near and far—including
our Monday night Acts2U group

and Gracie, woman's best girlfriend, who loves me
unconditionally

Contents

Introduction

Girlfriends are a feminine necessity—so is girl time!

A friend is someone who sees through you

and still enjoys the view.

Wilma Askinas

U m, honey . . . ?" my sweet, Renaissance-man husband, Michael, has been known to say on occasion—especially some hormonally charged ones—"I think you need a little girl time."

All women do.

Although we love and adore the men in our lives, without our girlfriends, we'd be lost. Their friendships sustain us. They rejoice in our successes, share in our sorrows, cry with us, pray for us, laugh with us, and just plain old *listen* to us as we go on and on and on about something that's bothering us.

Most men I know—even the sensitive guy I married—glaze over after about half an hour.

Tops.

I NEED my girlfriend time. I start to go into withdrawal if I go too long without it. And it's not pretty.

Whether it's going out to lunch and a movie with my best friend Lana, dropping by my dear friend Pat's for a nice cuppa tea and evening chat, or talking on the phone for hours to my Southern-fried friend Annette, my girl time is a feminine necessity. A precious one.

It is to every woman.

We women have a connection, an inexplicable bond that men simply can't share.

10

And talking is a huge part of that. With liberal doses of chocolate thrown in.

That's why since long before we were born there have been countless ladies' clubs—book clubs, garden clubs, bridge clubs, tea groups, Bible studies, or quilting bees. We women need our girl time to share our joys and struggles and to just plain old have some fun and let our hair down.

More than fifty years ago in our small Wisconsin town, my great-grandma started the Matson Family Club as a place for the women in the family and a few of the neighbor ladies to get together once a month for some afternoon coffee and a game of bingo—without men. Although most of the original club members (like my Great-Grandma Matson and my Grandma Florence) are long gone, their descendants, including my Aunt Sharon and Aunt Kathy still carry on the monthly tradition—only they meet in the evening now instead of in the afternoon.

My twenty-something Michigan friend Leona says she gets together with a group of five girlfriends—ages twenty-three to fifty—about once a month. "We play cards or board games, go out to dinner, or even take special trips," she said. "We always spend some time sharing about what's going on in our lives, and often we pray, right then, for each other. Two women are single, and three are married. It's a great way to encourage each other and have a blast, too."

Girl time is a wonderful time of encouragement, yet it

also allows us to talk, and sometimes vent—about our jobs, husbands, children, or difficult situations in our lives.

I remember years ago when I job-shared a secretarial position with a woman named Lisa. She worked mornings and I worked afternoons, with an hour overlap at lunch. We became fast friends during that hour, in which we each took turns saying to the other, "Can I vent?" before sharing a personal or work frustration with what we knew would be a kind and sympathetic ear.

We all need a safe place to voice our fears, concerns, or disappointments and to seek advice and prayer. It's an important girl bonding time.

Shopping is another great girlfriend bonding activity.

"Our favorite shopping activity is trying on formal dresses at pricey stores and then taking pictures of ourselves in the dressing room to impress our friends later," says my twenty-four-year-old colleague Heather. "Yeah, it's a little tacky, but it's fun!"

I enjoyed clothes shopping with girlfriends when I was younger, but now that I have my middle-age spread thing goin' on, I prefer browsing through antique malls and bookstores instead. That way I don't have to confront those awful mirrors and unflattering lights and can still enjoy my chocolate afterwards—guilt free.

It doesn't matter whether you shop, do lunch, go to the movies, chat on the phone, or join a book club. What *does* matter is taking the time—no, *making* the time—for your girlfriends.

Oh, and one more thing: Don't forget the chocolate.

> On the path between the homes of friends, grass does not grow.
>
> *Norwegian Proverb*

1

Not-So-Divine Secrets of the Blah-Blah Sisterhood

We may not have cut our fingers and mixed our blood in a stealthy nighttime ritual, but we're a sisterhood of friends nonetheless. Just call us the Blah-Blah Sisterhood.

Good communication is as stimulating as black coffee, and just as hard to sleep after.

Anne Morrow Lindbergh

Stealthily we made our way through the warehouse, foraging for food and necessary supplies to get us through the long, cold night. Silent and with all our senses on alert we slunk past the sentries, afraid of getting caught.

"Hey, what are you doing?"

Uh-oh. Now we were in for it.

"Hi, Lana and Laura," said Kevin from our church singles group as we rounded the frozen-food aisle of the discount warehouse store. "Whatcha got there?"

"Um, oh nothing," I said as Lana tried to shield our cart from view.

Too late I realized we hadn't planned our strategy properly. *I* should have been the one protecting the grocery cart. Lana was too little. Her petite form only blocked the upper right-hand corner.

"Let's see here . . . popcorn, potato chips, pizza rolls, chocolate, Twinkies, soda, candy bars, ice-cream sandwiches, Ben & Jerry's . . . Gee, looks like you're stocking up for the winter," Kevin smirked.

"No, we're having some girls—some *young* girls—over for a slumber party," I retorted.

16

"Oh, wow. That's really nice of you . . . Is it like one of those Big Sister things?"

"Something like that," I said. "Well, gotta go now, Kevin, or we'll be late. See ya later."

"Whew. That was close," Lana said as we loaded up our trunk in the parking lot. "I didn't want any of the guys we know to see us with all this junk food. We'd never hear the end of it. But we shouldn't have lied to Kevin . . ."

"We didn't lie. We *are* having some young girls over—Michelle's only eighteen, you know. And we *are* like her big sister . . . Besides, one of the other girls is bringing her younger sister over, too. I think she's just twenty or twenty-one, and she's had kind of a rough past and feels a little uncomfortable about coming here. Blah, blah, blah . . ."

Thus began a sisterhood of friends. The Blah-Blah Sisterhood.

Thus began a sisterhood of friends. The Blah-Blah Sisterhood.

We had a great time that night at the slumber party in our apartment—this group of about a dozen single women from our nondenominational church—playing a little Amy Grant on the stereo, munching on junk food, talking about guys, and especially, opening up our hearts and our lives.

At one point, we all sat in a circle and shared our life stories. As each woman shared her mostly G-rated story—raised in a good Christian home, grew up going to church but the church was pretty dead, blah, blah, blah—I could see my friend's younger sister (the one with the rough past) start to squirm and grow more and more uncomfortable.

Wanting to be a good hostess and put her at ease, I raised my hand. "Can I go next?"

And then I plunged in and proceeded to share the *Reader's Digest* condensed version of my oh-so-colorful, wild-and-crazy, X-rated past. When I finished, a couple of the girls' mouths were hanging open, but my new friend was smiling and visibly relaxed.

"Well, I can top *that*," she said with a laugh.

We became fast friends that night, and a few years later she was a bridesmaid in my wedding. In fact, she and her husband—she later married a great guy from our singles group—were instrumental in getting Michael and me together.

It's wonderful to have a sisterhood of friends you can confide in, share secrets with, and just do plain good old-fashioned girl stuff with.

Although Lana was in her late twenties and I'd just passed the thirty-year mark when we had that infamous slumber party, it was like we were carefree teenagers again that night as we curled each other's hair, painted our toenails, gave each other facials, and giggled over bad blind dates—all while in our fun pj's and bunny slippers.

Could you see guys doing that?

Well . . . maybe the bunny slipper part. They don't know what they're missing with all that hunting, fishing, and camping outdoors stuff.

Give me a good slumber party any day. No bugs, no dirt, and flushable bathroom facilities.

Another time, three of us from the "sisterhood," Michelle, Lana, and I, got together and planned a fun surprise for our friend Pat's birthday.

Now, Pat's nearly a decade older than me—and I was about the oldest in the group—and at the time the only married one among us. Therefore, she didn't feel the need to go out gallivanting every weekend the way we did and liked nothing more than to stay at home and relax with her sweetie—a concept we couldn't identify with. We were always teasing her and telling her she needed to get out more and not lead such a boring, fuddy-duddy life.

We learned that this fuddy-duddyness even extended to her pajamas.

Her sleepwear of choice was long, flannel nightgowns or pajamas. And as single women longing to get married and have romantic nights with our husbands, we couldn't understand why she didn't wear pretty, sexy lingerie for her husband, Ken.

So we made up a little song for her and serenaded her at her party.

She wore white flannel (whoa, whoa)
High-necked, long-sleeved, and to the floor (whoa, whoa,
    whoa)
She likes to burrow and stay warm—through the night
Ken has waited for ye-ars, hoping tonight is the night
She'll leave the flannel behind—
Satin and lace, and not a trace
Of white flannel (whoa, whoa . . .)
Someday he'll see his dream come true (whoa, whoa, whoa)
'Til then, he'll just have to make do
With her socks, too . . .

Our song was the hit of the party. And it was only many years later—when we were all married with husbands of our own—that Pat revealed that she *did* in fact have a drawerful of satin and lace at home. Always had. And much of it was even red. "I just didn't want to make you girls 'stumble,'" she said with a sly smile.

I take back everything I ever said about her being a fuddy-duddy.

And now that I'm over forty and have been married several years, I can see the fuddy-duddy attraction. Only now some of *my* young friends don't get it and think I lead a boring, blah life.

I prefer to think of it as blah-blah.

Long before I ever heard of the Ya-Ya Sisterhood, I was the queen of the blah-blahs. When I write a book, my fingers fly over the keyboard—I type a hundred words a minute—as I

20

compose my chapters, and then periodically I'll run into a sentence or a paragraph that's not quite what I want to say, or I'm not sure exactly WHAT I want to say there yet, but not wanting to lose my writing momentum I'll just write "blah-blah" and highlight it in yellow to remind myself that I need to come back and fix it later.

This is what I call the blah-blah factor.

The blah-blah factor isn't limited to just writing, though. I use it often when speaking to my friends: "And then do you know what he did? Blah, blah, blah . . ." And I thought I was the only blah-blah woman out there.

But then my friend Jan told me that she and some other girlfriends went to see *The Divine Secrets of the Ya-Ya Sisterhood,* and afterward when they were at Jan's house talking away, one of them said, "We're not the Ya-Yas, we're the Blah-Blahs, 'cause all we do is talk."

I hear that. As does my friend Katie, who became a first-time mom to a newborn when she was forty-seven.

Katie has a twin sister, Carol, who's her best friend. And when the two of them get together, it's quite the gab fest. One day when Carol was visiting and she and Katie were in the midst of one of their lengthy sisterly conversations, little Jacqueline—who was just ten months old at the time—was listening intently, her eyes going back and forth between the two sisters, when she suddenly piped up with, "Blah, blah, blah."

Jacqueline's now the youngest member of the Blah-Blah Sisterhood.

A faithful friend is an image of God.

French Proverb

Girl Pearls Organize a fun slumber party with five or six of your girlfriends and pretend you're back in high school again—eating junk food, playing your favorite songs, polishing each other's toenails, and, of course, talking about "boys"!

2

The Ladies Who Lunch

An hour lunch is never enough time to catch
up with girlfriends—that's only an appetizer.
The waiter knows when he sees us coming that
it's going to be at least a three-hour tour.

The growth of true friendship
may be a lifelong affair.

Sarah Orne Jewett

My sister-in-law Sheri has been having lunch with the same quartet of women for more than twenty years.

It's a tradition.

She first met two of the women, Doreen and Karen, in a church singles group when she was in her mid-twenties. A little later, after she was married and six months pregnant with twins, Sheri met the fourth member of their quartet, Barbara (Karen's sister, also the mother of twins), at a retreat.

Over twenty years ago, the four women individually went to a women's conference one February and decided to go out for lunch at the nearby TGI Friday's, where they had a great time talking and laughing.

They got together a couple times later that year for lunch and then decided to plan a special Christmas lunch—just the four of them—at the same TGI Friday's where they'd first bonded months before.

And so a tradition was born.

For the past twenty-four years, the four friends have met for a fun Christmas lunch at the same restaurant and exchanged gifts.

One year Karen, the single woman in the group, who always likes to create a party atmosphere, brought some festive Christmas mugs and napkins for the women to use. And so another tradition was born. Every year since, Karen has brought the same mugs and napkins to TGI Friday's. (Well, not the *exact* same napkins—by now they'd have taken on a life of their own.)

The women have certain rituals they observe every year: They always sit in the corner at the same table, "the Tiffany table,"—a pretty round table with inlaid glass. "One time a graduation party had come in and took our table, and we were quite upset," Sheri said. "So now one of us always gets there really early to claim our table in advance."

Each woman in the quartet buys the same three items to give to the others, so that everyone goes home with the same gifts. (For example, Sheri might buy three identical sets of stationery for her friends, while Barbara might buy three boxes of candy.) "And we always make Doreen order first 'cause she'd always pick what someone else was having," Sheri said.

Karen also brings a bag of candy for their server.

The servers—who are different every year—always get to hear the women's lunch-tradition story and "are always nice." The women will have coffee or soda to start, then enjoy their main course, and then linger over dessert. "We're there for a couple hours at least, usually longer," said Sheri, "but we're in the corner, so we really don't bother anybody."

Plus, the ladies always make sure to tip generously.

The group even has an unofficial name: the BDK Group.

"That's my fault," said Sheri. "I'd always put 'Lunch with BDK' (Barbara, Doreen, and Karen) on my calendar when we were scheduled to meet, so it's simply become that over the years." The others tried to work in different variations with the initials so Sheri wouldn't be left out, but it sounded awkward and didn't have quite the same ring to it, especially to Sheri's ears, so upon her insistence, it remained the BDK Group.

In addition to their annual Christmas luncheon, the four women meet at least four or five times a year for lunch and a movie just for fun.

"We have to find a movie that nobody's seen and everyone wants to see, which is sometimes hard," Sheri said. "So we don't always go to a movie—we just spend longer talking. Or sometimes we'll go to Doreen's and have a potluck and watch movies on her widescreen TV, or we'll take turns making lunch. But we always get together during the day so the husbands aren't left out."

For birthdays, the ladies always like to lunch at the Olive Garden.

The friends' foursome is exclusive, but for the best of reasons. "Who wants to join a bunch of old ladies who have been doing something for twenty years?" Sheri said. "They'd feel like an outsider."

My best friend Lana and I don't go to lunch as often as we'd like, due to our different schedules and commitments. However, we try to get together at least every other month for

26

lunch and a matinee. Sometimes the lunch is at an elegant tea room; other times it's just pizza or Chinese. The main thing is to have time talking together and connecting. We always laugh, and sometimes cry, but are always thankful for the deep friendship God has given us.

When I worked in an office, I always tried to go out to lunch at least once or twice a week with girlfriends—either coworkers or friends who lived nearby. But now that I work out of my home, it takes more of an effort to make that happen. I can get pretty isolated if I'm not careful.

That's why my writing pal Jan—who also works at home—and I have made a pact to get together for lunch once a month or at least every other month. She lives about thirty miles away, so we usually meet midway at our favorite Chili's where we'll talk for hours over Caesar salad or chicken tacos, sharing our writing hopes and joys or encouraging and lifting one another up over rejections and disappointments.

The main thing is to have time talking together and connecting.

Although I enjoy fine dining, my writer's budget doesn't usually allow for going out to an expensive restaurant for lunch. So sometimes I'll invite a friend over to my house and try to create an elegant atmosphere at home instead.

I'll set the table with my best linens, china, and crystal, and—depending on the season—I'll serve a light quiche and salad or homemade soup and crusty bread. Unfortunately, although I love to cook, I don't always have the time to make something from scratch, but I'm fortunate to have a Trader Joe's (a wonderful gourmet and organic foods discount store) nearby, where I can pick up frozen stuffed salmon or crab cakes, pop them into the oven, and serve them along with a lovely Caesar or spinach salad, followed by fresh berries and cream or something yummy and chocolaty and decadent.

Other times I'll do a simple afternoon tea.

Sometimes I'll make a couple kinds of sandwiches (Michael and I discovered a delicious sandwich of cheddar cheese and green apple between thick buttered slices of whole-grain farm bread when we visited Yorkshire, so I'll often serve a lighter version of that), scones with jam and cream, and a small, yummy sweet such as a dense chocolate truffle. Other times I'll serve puff pastry with seafood filling, piping hot mushroom turnovers (Trader Joe's to the rescue again), and assorted tea breads—lemon poppy seed, pumpkin, or banana (no nuts)—and lemon squares or chocolate-dipped strawberries.

My friend feels cosseted and cared for, and we've both enjoyed a delicious lunch at a fraction of the cost.

I especially like to do this for friends who are going through a rough time, because for an hour or two they can forget their difficulties and simply enjoy a relaxed, pampering lunch and a nice hot cup of tea and sympathy.

Like my British friends over in Merrie Olde England, I

firmly believe there's nothing like a soothing cuppa hot tea to lift your spirits and make you feel better (my tea of choice is PG Tips, which you can find at Cost Plus or any English specialty store). William Gladstone, prime minister of England in the late 1800s, said it best: "If you are cold, tea will warm you—if you are heated, it will cool you—if you are depressed, it will cheer you—if you are excited, it will calm you."

My friend Pat belongs to a women's tea group that's been meeting once a month for the past seven years for gracious and lovely luncheon teas that usually last two to three hours.

Pat and her friend Gaylene, who both love tea and the wonderful ritual associated with it, started the group of six when they worked together. They were looking for ladies who take pleasure in preparing special food and entertaining elegantly. "One month we go to someone's house in the tea group; the other month we try to go *out* somewhere for tea," Pat said. That way each member only hosts one tea a year at her home.

My friend feels cosseted and cared for, and we've both enjoyed a delicious lunch at a fraction of the cost.

Scones are always a part of tea, as are the sweets for dessert. And each hostess gets to choose whether she'll have the traditional sandwiches—cucumber, chicken salad, smoked salmon, and the like—or perhaps something warm, like quiche.

Pat, who lived in England for several years, has introduced some English favorites at her teas, such as sausage rolls (puff pastry with sausage inside), Scotch eggs (hard-boiled egg inside sausage, breaded and fried), sherry trifle, and sticky toffee pudding.

"The focus of the tea is the ceremony and the elegance and intimacy of it," Pat explained. "We talk about everything—politics, religion, family, gardens, trips, books—and everybody doesn't always agree (we have some very strong personalities in our tea group), but we all get along, so it's really nice. We all enjoy getting away from the hurried pace of life, so we never rush our teas."

Everyone in the group also enjoys decorating for the tea and takes great pains to make her event as beautiful as possible for the others. For instance, one of the women held a winter tea where everything was silver and white: white lace tablecloth, silver-and-white confetti atop white china, silver-and-white tiered servers, white flowers in the center of the table, dark pink roses in small vases at each place setting for a splash of color, delicate white snowflakes and crystal prisms hanging from the chandeliers, and white candelabra with white-frosted candles.

Some of the women are china collectors, so they will have a different place setting for each woman. And there are always beautiful, fresh flowers.

30

Which is more than they can say for some of the tea places they've ventured out to.

"One time we thought we were going to a really nice tea at an old English hotel in San Francisco," recalled Pat.

Not exactly.

The flowers were dead, the tablecloths were dirty, the food was dreadful, the tea was lukewarm, and to top it all off, the server was wearing a dirty apron. The ladies didn't stay long.

Another time the whole group went down to Los Angeles and bunked at Pat's sister Julie's before heading out for tea the next afternoon at a noted historical garden, which unfortunately, turned out to be another disappointment. The food was "okay," but the women were dismayed to be right in the middle of the beautiful rose garden without a single live flower anywhere in the whole tea room.

At another tea house, the ladies were greeted with bare midriffs and piercings "in parts that hurt" (navels, lips, etc.), Pat recalled. Ambience was not the specialty there.

"We've found that we prefer to go to somebody's house—all of which have beautiful yards and gardens—by far," Pat said. "Then we're never disappointed."

The ladies are very particular about what constitutes a proper tea—a beautiful setting, wonderful ambience, nice (and clean) linens and china, excellent food—just the right mix of savory and sweet—and always, always, a piping *hot* pot of tea.

Nothing spoils an afternoon tea faster than tepid, too-weak, or too-strong tea.

Brewing the perfect pot of tea is an art form unto itself, but the ladies in Pat's group are up to the task.

Many aren't.

Not just the tea-brewing part, but the entire ritual. Tea is not something that can be microwaved, thrown together at the last minute, or grabbed on the go. Afternoon tea is all about beauty, about slowing down and taking time to appreciate the finer things in life.

Time spent with girlfriends—eating and talking—is one of the finer things in life. Whether it's over a leisurely, picture-perfect afternoon tea or over your favorite pizza, it's the gabbing, the listening, the sharing, and the laughing that makes for a perfect repast.

> It is that my friends have made the story of my life.
> In a thousand ways they have turned my limitations
> into beautiful privileges, and enabled me to walk
> serene and happy in the shadow cast by my
> deprivation.
>
> *Helen Keller*

Girl Pearls Why not host a best friends tea at your home? Invite two or three of your girlfriends and have each one of them invite their best friend to a lovely afternoon tea.

The initial three or four friends—including you—can make the sandwiches, scones, and dessert, while the best-friend invitees can just relax and enjoy themselves. (I confess I stole this idea from my best friend Lana's coworker Julie, whose delightful girlfriends tea I attended a few years ago. Thanks, Julie!)

3

Soul Sisters

She's a genteel Southerner; I'm a direct, to-the-point Yankee. She's from the inner city of Detroit; I'm a white-bread girl from small-town Wisconsin. And yet our friendships thrive. How opposites attract and complement one another in friendships.

Accept one another, then, just as Christ accepted you, in order to bring praise to God.

Romans 15:7

What happens when you take a genteel, soft-spoken Southern woman and a laid-back but direct California girl—who was born and raised a Yankee—and put them together?

In the case of me and my Texas pal Annette, or as I call her, my "southern-fried friend," they form a deep and lasting friendship. And laugh like crazy whenever they get together—especially at their Yankee/Southerner differences.

I love Annette. She's become a dear, precious, and fun friend. But that doesn't mean we'll ever see eye to eye on certain geographic customs.

Although I was born and raised in Wisconsin, which qualifies me for Yankee status, I've now lived in the Golden State for more than twenty years, which officially qualifies me as a California girl, albeit a northern California girl.

Not at all the same thing as a southern California girl.

The quintessential southern California girl usually sports sun-streaked long blond hair and a golden tan and spends a lot of time in bikinis, shorts, or skimpy sundresses, whereas the northern California girl has more of that earthy, natural, laid-back hippie kind of thing going for her.

Although I may not wear tie-dyed shirts and Birkenstocks, I do go barelegged all year long (yes, I still shave my legs)

36

and only wear makeup when I absolutely *have* to. I can't remember the last time I wore nylons. (Or as Southern women say, "hose").

And I don't plan to put them on anytime soon.

My southern-fried friend Annette and I first met at a book convention luncheon a few years ago. But it wasn't until we'd both read one another's books and formed a mutual admiration sisterhood that we became fast friends.

Wow, can that woman write! Annette's a natural-born storyteller. Her book *Watermelon Days and Firefly Nights,* with its eccentric but delightful small-town Texas characters, is a particular favorite of mine.

Although we're different in many ways—she has kids, and I don't; she's a registered nurse, and I can't stand the sight of blood; she likes cooked turnip greens, and I don't even know exactly what they are but can't stand the sound or thought of 'em—we share some of the same passions: reading, writing, Anne Lamott, and Jesus.

I'd assumed the northern California–bred Lamott might be a little too, um, earthy for a sweet Texas Christian girl like Annette. But I discovered Annette likes her for the very same reasons I do. Ms. Lamott is an incredibly gifted writer and a born-again believer who loves Jesus. She's also painfully honest and REAL and not afraid to show her flaws and shortcomings—even when that garners criticism from other believers. Annette and I both loved her wonderful *Traveling*

Mercies and each keep a copy of her inspiring writer's primer, *Bird by Bird,* close at hand.

But back to my Texas friend.

When I went to Fort Worth for a speaking engagement a couple years ago, Annette graciously offered to drive me around—even though we still didn't know each other that well—and to "man" my book table at my speaking event.

That's really where our friendship began.

After that trip, when we realized we shared some mutual passions, we began e-mailing and calling each other regularly, and in time I persuaded her to come out for a visit—her first time in California—for a much-needed writing getaway. (My kind writing friend Jan graciously let us use her lovely home for our "retreat" while she and her husband were on vacation.)

Annette was delighted with the beautiful foothills of the Sierra Nevadas, and we enjoyed a delicious dinner at a local restaurant, chatting long into the night after we returned "home."

The next morning, as I stumbled out of bed in my rumpled sweats and bed head and headed down the hall toward the kitchen for a cup of tea, I passed the open bathroom door and noticed Annette.

Completely dressed and bent over, teasing her hair. When she straightened up, I saw that she had a full face of make-up on.

38

"Where are you going?" I asked.

"Nowhere."

"Are you expecting someone?"

"No."

"Then why do you have makeup on?"

"Y'all wouldn't want to *see* me without makeup!"

That's when I realized that we were from completely different worlds.

"No Southern girl goes to the post office without her makeup on," Annette explained. "Appearance is a huge thing. It's very important for a Southern girl to look feminine."

> *"No Southern girl goes to the post office without her makeup on."*

"But we're not *going* to the post office—or *any*where for that matter," I said. "We're staying here inside the house, just you and me, to write."

"I know. But I'd feel naked without it."

Well, you can certainly tell *I'm* not from the South. If I put on makeup every time I went to the post office—two or three times a week—I'd never have time to get anything done. Besides, my favorite postal clerk wouldn't recognize me. He's accustomed to seeing me come rushing in with flyaway hair, packages sliding out from under my sweats-clad arms, dark circles under my makeup-free eyes, baggy sweatpants, and bare feet shoved hurriedly into loafers.

Annette wouldn't be caught dead in loafers and sweats.

Intrigued, over breakfast that morning I asked her to clue me in a little on the southern way of life—starting with the way women dress.

She was happy to oblige and began with accessories.

"Excess is never enough," Annette said. "If you wear a watch, you wear a bracelet."

"On the same wrist?" I asked, confused.

"Oh, no. On opposite arms. It's all about balance. And we would sooner go without a bra than without earrings," she declared.

Then Annette revealed something she'd hesitated to mention before, but now that we were such good friends and were having this great girl bonding time, she finally felt at liberty to share. "I was shocked that day when you spoke to the women's group in Texas and you didn't have earrings on," she confided.

"Yes, I did. I always wear earrings to my speaking engagements."

"Well they weren't big enough then, 'cause I couldn't see them," she said.

In Texas bigger is always better.

"I do remember that you had a naked wrist that day, though," she said.

"A *naked* wrist? Oh, that's right—I remember. My watch had broken earlier on the plane."

40

"Well, if you're not going to wear a watch, you *have* to wear a bracelet," she teased. "Accessories are a huge thing in the South."

"You mean like scarves?"

"Not scarves. That's a Yankee thing. I'm talkin' jewelry," Annette continued in her soft Texas twang, with barely a pause. "Most Southern women are huge diamond people— although I'm really not. But you'd *never* have a naked hand. Very rarely will you see a Southern woman without at least one ring on each hand—and many of them would have one on every finger.

"You always want balance," she stressed, "a ring and a watch, or a ring on each hand."

And here I'd always thought that great line in *Steel Magnolias*—"What sets us apart from the animals is our ability to accessorize"—was just a funny exaggeration for the movies. Now, thanks to Annette and some of my other southern-fried friends, I've since realized it's the gospel truth.

"Highlights are pretty much a must in our hair," Annette said, "and as the former Texas governor Ann Richards always said, 'We wear big hair 'cause it makes our hips look smaller.'"

That's my problem. If only I'd known about the big-hair principle sooner, I wouldn't have had to spend so much time—and money—camouflaging my hips with long sweaters and jackets.

On a little southern-beauty overload, and needing to get to work, I asked Annette if we could continue my southern-fried education later.

She graciously, and apologetically, acquiesced, as any good Southern woman would do.

That's another thing I've discovered about women from the South: Good manners are of the utmost importance. Southerners value gentility, charm, and politeness. "You can say anything about anybody as long as you say, 'bless her heart . . .'" Annette explained.

"Southerners aren't as blunt as Northerners," she continued over dinner later. "We kind of have to warm up to conversations. We'll say, 'How's your mama? How's your grandma? How's the weather?' We have to do all these nicety-nice things before we get to the meat of the conversation—even in business."

Hmmm. I don't know if I'd have the patience for that.

I'm more direct—preferring to cut straight to the chase, especially in business dealings, while Annette would have to "kind of sidle up to the issue, in general."

"We don't want to hurt anybody's feelings," she said. "Southern women are all about charm and sweetness and gentleness," Annette explained. "We may be tough as nails and get what we want, but by the time we get through with you, you'll think it's *your* idea."

Gosh, and all along I'd thought most everything we'd done

42

together *had* been my idea. This conversation was indeed enlightening.

Annette continued: "We revere old ladies," she said. "Almost every family is run by some old woman—usually an aunt or a grandma. We love her, but we're a little scared of her, too. My dad always said about my grandma, 'If Mother had had an education, she would have been dangerous.'"

Part of that reverence extends to their loved ones' appearance.

"It's very important that we not let our old women get to lookin' ugly," Annette said. "We see that they have nice house shoes and plenty of Estée Lauder bath powders, and that they keep perms in their hair even if they only leave the house to go to the doctor's. I promised my mom, and my daughter Rachel's promised me, that when we get old and can't see our chin hairs, we'll pluck them for each other."

I may not be southern, but Mom, I, Laura, also hereby promise to pluck your chin hairs when you're older—should they ever sprout on your pretty face. Bless your heart.

Next, Annette launched into the care and feeding of Southern men.

"Even though we've had a female governor of Texas, to be a bossy woman is a bad thing," she cautions. "Southern men are real traditional, so Southern women have a way of working around that—to make the men think it's their idea even when it isn't. The husband's still the head of the house—or we still let him think he is. It's like the line in *My Big Fat Greek Wedding* where the mother tells the daughter, 'The man may be the head of the household, but the woman is the neck.'"

Southern women are definitely the neck.

I'll never forget one day when I was talking on the phone to Annette and I was complaining about something Michael hadn't done—which I planned to discuss with him when he got home from work that night.

> "Bless his heart. He can't help it that he's a man. That's just the way they are."

And my southern-fried friend took me to task.

"Now you be sweet to that man," Annette lectured. "He's had a hard day. Bless his heart. He can't help it that he's a man. That's just the way they are."

Sounds like the lyric to a song . . .

Cooking and hospitality are also a big deal in the South. So is Velveeta cheese.

"No gathering is complete without the Ro-tel cheese dip," Annette declared. "You mix a can of Ro-tel tomatoes and a half block of Velveeta. If you want to make it gourmet, you chop up an onion."

Now *that* I already knew firsthand from my husband. When Michael and I were dating, he brought over this great cheese dip for a potluck one night. "Yum, what IS this?" I asked, biting into another ooey-gooey mouthful.

44

"Ro-tel cheese dip," Michael answered with a proud Texas swagger. "Ah picked it up when ah was living in Houston."

That's another geographic difference between my southern friend and me—our state's approach to health. California is renowned for its abundance of fresh fruits and vegetables and healthy sprouted lifestyle.

"If you want to be health conscious in Texas, you either scrape a carrot or slice up an apple," Annette said.

"*Scrape* a carrot?"

"Why? What do y'all say?" she asked.

"*Peel* a carrot."

"No, ma'am! You peel a 'tater, but you scrape a carrot."

Healthiness aside, I learned cornbread is the bread of choice in the South, and favorite foods include fried catfish, a nice thick steak, and chicken-fried steak.

"For lunch we often go to Cracker Barrel, because they have good greens," Annette said.

"Salad?" I ask.

"No, *greens.* Turnip greens. You cook those babies 'til there's no life left in 'em and you serve 'em with pot liquor."

"Pot liquor?"

"The juice from the greens (turnip or mustard) seasoned with ham or ham hocks."

I don't even know what a ham hock is.

Another southern thing is black-eyed peas. On New Year's Day, Texans always eat black-eyed peas—to ensure that the upcoming year will be prosperous. "If you don't eat them all year long, you at least have to have a tablespoon for prosperity on New Year's," Annette said. "It's bad luck not to. Story goes, when the Yankees came through and destroyed all the southern people's crops, they didn't recognize the peas as being people food. They thought it was for the livestock," she explained. "Southerners who'd been ravaged by the Yankees during the war survived by eating their crops of black-eyed peas. So now we eat them so we will have a prosperous year."

Southerners also say things with more words than are necessary.

"Not 'Where are you going?' but 'Where are you going *to*?'" Annette said. "Not 'Put it on the shelf,' but 'Put it *up* on the shelf.' Almost any phrase we can stick extra words into, we will."

They also have their own peculiarly southern vocabulary: "We *carry* people to the doctor, and we say 'I'm fixin' to go' . . . or 'I don't reckon we'll go today . . .'" Annette said.

Isn't that just the cutest thing? Bless her heart. As you can tell, my southern-fried friend has had a gracious impact on me.

But Annette, that still doesn't mean I'm fixin' to wear makeup around the house.

My girlfriend Toni and I met when we worked together on the college newspaper.

She was streetwise, urban, black, and hip, born and raised in Detroit's inner city. And I was a prissy, proper white girl from the California suburbs—by way of small-town Wisconsin.

We bonded because we were the two oldest in the class. Everyone else was eighteen or nineteen and fresh out of high school, while we were in our thirties. Correction. Toni was in her late twenties; I was in my early thirties. Toni and I had virtually nothing in common except our shared love of writing and our seriousness about getting our college degrees.

Yet we became close friends.

"You and I loved each other to death," Toni recalled recently when we were catching up on the phone, "but we had no common interests. You came from a completely different area than me and didn't know a whole lot of black people. But then, I didn't know a whole lot of white people. I always described the white picket fence scenario, thinking that was the white folks world. We both shared some generalities about the other's race."

The first time Toni really noticed our differences was at a community college journalism conference. "We were sitting in the hotel room talking while I was doing my hair and you asked me, 'Why are you ironing your hair?'" Toni recalled. "And I said, 'We don't call it ironing; we call it curling.'" (Toni's curling iron looked unlike any I'd ever seen, and every time she curled—which looked more like ironing or straightening to me—smoke rose out of the ultra-hot iron.)

Toni and I had other noticeable differences, too: She was married with kids; I was single and longing to be married. She liked bloody, action-packed shoot 'em ups; I liked talky English chick flicks. She liked to decorate with chrome and glass; I preferred old wood and china.

"Your house made me think of the little old grandmas on TV with all the teacups and doilies and lace," Toni said. "You had an unwritten book of etiquette, attitude, and language that I knew nothing about and had only heard on TV," she said, remembering the first time I told her I was "going to tea" with friends. "I thought tea was something you drank when you were sick," she said, laughing. "The idea of 'going to tea' was foreign. You *go* to a party, you *go* to the bathroom."

In time, though, Toni *came* to tea at my little cottage and loved it.

But that was many, many months after we'd become friends at the newspaper.

I was the editor-in-chief of the college paper; Toni was my entertainment editor, and part of her job was to write reviews of plays and movies. So one time, the two of us went to see August Wilson's *Fences* on opening night and attended the reception afterwards.

It was Toni's first entertainment review, let alone reception, and she was a little intimidated.

"I figured you had a whole lot more culture than I did, so I'd stick close to you," Toni recalled. "You were trying to make me feel comfortable, so you took me over to the food table. When we got to the paté, I said loudly, 'What is THAT?'"

"Shhh," I answered my culture-shocked friend. "It's paté. Just watch me and eat it the way I do."

"I'm not eatin' *that!*"

Toni also refused to touch the guacamole—"I don't eat anything that's green," she declared.

At a loss, I wasn't sure what to do, and then Toni spotted two servers and headed in their direction, explaining her dilemma.

They fixed her right up.

"Girl, trust me, you can eat this," one said, pointing to a puff-pastry appetizer.

"Here, try this, girlfriend. You'll like it," the other one chimed in.

"How come you didn't listen to me when *I* told you?" I asked my friend.

"'Cause the sistas ain't gonna steer me wrong," Toni said.

"I wouldn't either. Besides, why can't *I* be your sister?"

"It's not an 'er' situation," Toni instructed me. "It's not 'sister,' it's 'sista.' It's not a sibling."

Toni was forever trying to educate me in street language. And I, who won spelling bees in school and cringe whenever I see a misspelled word *any*where—including billboards—tried to teach Toni how to spell certain words correctly.

"There's no *u* in rhythm," I told her one day in the newsroom as I proofed her article for mistakes.

"No, there's no 'you' in rhythm," Toni cracked, having seen me try to dance in her living room the night before.

Nobody in the newsroom ever forgot how to spell rhythm after that.

I'll never forget the time—in the late '80s—I came rushing into the newsroom all excited about an article I'd been assigned to write for the local paper where I was serving an internship.

"Toni, Toni, guess what? I get to write a story on teenagers who've left gangs and are trying to go straight. I'll even be interviewing some former gang members! But I've got this list of terms I need to learn before the interview. I figured out that 'hood means neighborhood, but I'm not exactly sure what crib or homeboy or any of these other words mean. Can you help me translate it, please?"

"Po' baby. It ain't gonna happen," Toni said, shaking her head at me affectionately. "They gone eat you alive. You will never be able to chop it up with the fellas. They will spit all kinds of knowledge at you. You will be forced to shake the spot with the quickness [translation: "leave in a hurry"]. Don't even try to hang."

Huh?

I remember the Sunday Toni came to services with me at my large, nondenominational, laid-back, mostly white church. During the sermon, she started talking back to the pastor. He'd preach an important point from Scripture, and while the rest of the congregation—including me—was nodding in silent agreement, Toni would call out, "Amen!" "All right now," or "Go 'head."

And yet, for all our differences of background and culture, Toni is my soul sister. Um, sista. We graduated from college together in 1992, and I keep a picture of us in our caps and gowns with proud journalism degrees clutched in hand on my bulletin board.

Lana is also my soul sister—although many don't immediately see our connection at first either.

"You and *Laura* are best friends?" an acquaintance asked Lana incredulously after getting to know her at an afternoon tea.

I can understand her surprise.

Lana's got both feet on the ground and is very pragmatic. When we first met, she had her college degree and had already been a teacher for a few years, while I had just a couple of college credits under my belt.

Lana's steady and practical.

I'm flighty (or used to be) and a dreamer.

Lana's petite and blonde.

I'm neither.

Lana's always perfectly groomed and manicured.

I bite my nails.

Lana's always up on the latest fashions and usually looks like she just stepped straight from the pages of *Vogue*.

I'm an ad for Sweats 'R Us.

Lana always drives a nice new car.

I've had only two cars in the sixteen years we've been friends.

Lana pumps iron.

I pump gas.

Lana's a sports fanatic.

I'm an ad for *Couch Potato Living*.

> *Lana pumps iron.*
> *I pump gas.*

Lana's had the same job for the past fifteen years.

I changed jobs almost as often as she changed clothes. (But that was until I found my calling—writing.)

Her new tea acquaintance couldn't see *what* we had in common.

Although it's not easily seen by the naked eye, under Lana's perfectly toned and my not-so-perfectly toned skin, we're soul sisters.

Lana and I were roommates when we were both single and relatively new Christians, slipping and stumbling our way through this whole new world of Christianity together, and that served to bond us for life. (Something about that whole "Do you think *he's* the one God's picked for me?" singles refrain we played over and over again so many nights in our apartment over Ben & Jerry's cookie-dough ice cream.)

Then there's the way she lovingly stepped up to the friendship plate when I was diagnosed with breast cancer just a year into my marriage. (I wrote about this in depth in *Thanks for the Mammogram!* but would like to give you the *Reader's Digest* condensed version here.)

A few days after my mastectomy, when I was released to go home from the hospital, I was still sore and tender from the surgery and wasn't moving very fast. Plus, I hadn't had a bath or shower in three days.

Can you say "attractive"?

That's when Lana came to visit, bearing gifts. After a few minutes, my best friend—who's never been shy—gently suggested that I needed a bath.

And so my five-foot-two, 105-pound friend—who's a teacher, not a nurse—helped her five-foot-seven, a little bit more than—okay, a lot more than—105-pound best friend into the tub.

I'm more grateful than I can say for my soul sisters—sistas.

> Once in an age, God sends to some of us a friend
> who loves in us . . . not the person that we are, but
> the angel we may be.

Harriet Beecher Stowe

Girl Pearls Do something that your soul sister likes to do—even if it's not your normal preference (i.e., hiking or camping). Be willing to try something new and different—like ham hocks or paté, perhaps. Or simply show her how much she means to you by going out of your way to do something thoughtful for her—like helping her wallpaper a bedroom or clean out the garage or bringing her breakfast or lunch when she's feeling under the weather.

4

It's All Relative

A look at the blessing of friendships
with women we're related to.

All the wealth in the world cannot be compared
with the happiness of living together happily united.

Margaret of Youville

Growing up, my cousin Kathy was very close to her year-and-a-half-younger sister, Joanne. They shared a bedroom with their older sister Lillie and spent many happy hours giggling over boys, makeup, and clothes.

So when Joanne—now married with kids and living in Montana—found out she needed a kidney transplant, Kathy—also married with kids but living in Minnesota—didn't hesitate for a moment to offer her kidney to her beloved sister.

Strong and healthy, Kathy assumed she'd be a good match, but when she was tested, her blood reacted against Joanne's, so she couldn't be a donor. "I was very disappointed," Kathy said, "as this was something I really wanted to be able to do for my sister."

Luckily, another sister was a match.

Bettie, who is seven years younger than Joanne and living in the same small Minnesota town as Kathy, had also gone in to be tested and was thrilled when she found out she was compatible and would be able to help her older sister.

But that didn't mean there weren't some butterflies.

Bettie was a little nervous about flying out to Spokane

(where the surgeries would take place). "It was hard to leave my children," she recalled.

Thankfully, the two sisters came through the surgeries with flying colors. The transplant center only did surgery on Thursdays, and the only date they could schedule would be on their older sister Lillie's birthday (Lillie had died years before.) "We both felt that it was the perfect day," Joanne says. "Nothing could go wrong; Lil was going to be with us."

Now it was time to recover.

By this time, all the other family members who'd gathered in Washington for the surgery had returned to their respective homes, so it was just Bettie, Joanne, and Joanne's husband, Rusty, together in a small apartment they'd rented near the hospital, where Rusty took care of the two sisters.

Bettie and Joanne both acknowledge that during their mutual recovery period they really got to know one another—which their age difference while growing up and then, later, geographic distance had precluded. Joanne left home at seventeen—when Bettie was only ten—to marry Rusty and move to Montana. Bettie also left home after high school, and since her husband was in the military, she moved frequently, so in the twenty-five years prior to the transplant, she probably saw Joanne only three or four times.

"The transplant provided us an opportunity to be with one another," Bettie said, "something that probably wouldn't have happened otherwise." The sisters were basically confined to the apartment, so they spent time talking about their lives, their children, their dreams, and their disappointments.

"Often we would get to remembering a family anecdote and laugh so hard that we physically hurt—our incisions were still quite painful—but we couldn't stop laughing, nor did we want to," Bettie says. "We had to find humor to help ease us along."

Bettie's flight home was December 23—just in time to be home with her own family for Christmas. "It was a tearful good-bye for Joanne and me," Bettie recalled. "We held each other and hugged for the longest time—didn't say much, just held each other. Rusty had to separate us or I would've missed boarding the plane."

Life is to be shared and appreciated, even across the miles.

Every year since the transplant, Joanne has sent Bettie flowers or balloons—something special to observe their surgery "anniversary."

"All of us seem to be so busy that sometimes we don't keep in touch with those we love and care so much about," said Joanne. "That's a lesson I have learned. Life is to be shared and appreciated, even across the miles. I am very blessed to have such wonderful, caring friends—my sisters."

Bettie is thankful for the time she and Joanne had together. "Even though there are many miles between us, some of my best memories are the ones we shared in that little apartment in Spokane," she said.

58

There are fewer miles between Bettie and Kathy now that they live in the same small Minnesota town.

"It's been really nice having her here sharing holidays and getting to know each others' families," Kathy said. The sisters take day trips to see some of the little towns nearby or go out to dinner and concerts. Plus, their daughters have become very good friends and do a lot together. As a result, the sisters have become quite close and "feel much more like family now."

My friend Pat's sister Julie was the youngest in the family—the "baby sister"—so they weren't all that close when they were young.

But now they're closer than ever.

"She's one of the most important people in the world to me," Pat said.

Julie lives in southern California, and Pat lives in northern California, so they take turns flying up and down the Golden State to see each other. They also talk on the phone several times a week.

The sisters have much in common: They both love to cook and decorate, enjoy reading and traveling—they often take trips together—and share a deep love of their families and each others' families. And now the fifty-something sisters have something else in common, too: grandbabies.

Pat and Julie have always been there for one another, particularly during the tough times.

My twenty-four-year-old twin nieces, Kari and Jennie, share that same kind of connection.

"We've always shared a special bond—even when we didn't get along," said Kari. "I could still always count on her, and she could count on me. There were times when I didn't like the choices Jennie was making, and she thought I could do better than the boyfriend I had, but we've never not loved each other."

There was a brief period, however, when the twins didn't *like* each other very much.

Jennie went through a rebellious phase when she was twenty, going out to clubs with a party crowd, staying away from church, and making some poor choices that resulted in negative consequences.

But then she met Jason.

"I was worried about some of the things from my past and how he'd react—wondering if he would reject me or keep me," Jennie recalled. "I was in my bedroom crying and Kari heard me, as she always does. She hugged me and let me cry on her shoulder. I kept saying, 'Why would he want me? I'm not good enough for him.' Kari was crying with me, and she said, 'Jennie, Jason would be lucky to have you. If he rejects you, then you know he isn't the right one. But if you like him, then you have to take this risk. You never know what could happen.'"

What happened is the young couple ended up getting

60

married and now have a beautiful baby daughter, Lexi. "Jason was worth the risk," Jennie said, "and I am grateful that Kari encouraged me to take such a huge leap."

Kari said she didn't realize how much she needed Jennie until she and her boyfriend, whom she'd been dating for three years and hoped to marry, broke up.

"When I got home late that night after he broke up with me, I was crying hysterically in my room," Kari recalled. "My mom was asleep, and my dad was getting ready to go to work, and I remember thinking, *I'm not going to call Jennie. I'm going to get through this on my own.* But my dad came in, and I was all curled up at the edge of the bed, crying really hard. I didn't want to wake up Mom, but Dad was worried about me, so he said, 'Call Jennie.'"

Even though it was now nearly one o'clock in the morning, Kari called her newly married sister—apologizing for waking her—sobbing and heartbroken. "What's *wrong* with me? What did I do wrong?" she wailed to her twin.

"It was different from any other time we'd talked," Kari said. "It wasn't like I was talking to my sister. I was talking to a sister, friend, and mom all in one. I knew if I could call my sister at one o'clock in the morning and be so upset and hyperventilating, that she'd be there for me—no matter what. I could count on her—she really truly meant it when she said, 'Anytime you need me, I'll be there.'

"Jennie's my best friend now," Kari said. "I can't picture my life without her."

Jennie feels the same way about her twin.

My sister Lisa and I aren't twins—she's fifteen months older than me—but when we were little, we looked a lot alike, so people often mistook us for twins. I still remember the neighborhood policeman in our small town who whenever he saw us would boom out, "Look out, here comes double trouble!"

When we were young, my sister and I were the best of friends. At night, we'd kneel by the side of our beds and say our "Now I lay me down to sleep . . ." prayers together, then go to sleep holding hands across the space between our twin beds.

As we grew older, we graduated into a big-girls' double bed complete with a pretty white chiffon coverlet and canopy dotted with lavender forget-me-nots. We loved that bed. Tucked in each night by our parents, we felt like fairy-tale princesses.

But a couple more years passed, and that bed became a battleground—complete with a clothesline down the center that the enemy (each other) wasn't allowed to cross.

In time, we grew up and made up.

And today we both know that we would be there in a heartbeat for one another if needed.

Lisa demonstrated this very tangibly when I had breast

cancer and was going through my difficult chemotherapy treatments. Since she has a medical background, she was very helpful in those early days of fear and confusion, explaining things to me in laymen's terms. She also came over every day after I was released from my hospital chemo treatments to give me the special shots I needed to bring my white counts back up to normal.

That's something I'll never forget. Thanks, Lee (that's Lisa's nickname). I love you. And though I'm not too good with needles, if you ever need one of my kidneys, it's yours.

> A friend is always a friend,
> and relatives are born to share our troubles.
>
> *Proverbs 17:17 CEV*

Girl Pearls If you live in the same town as your relative friends, consider trying to meet for breakfast once a week—or once a month, whatever your schedule allows—at your favorite bakery or café where you can sit and talk over croissants and coffee or hot chocolate. And if you don't live close by, schedule a weekly girl time gabfest on the phone instead. You could also band together to help out a worthy cause: walk in the annual American Cancer Society's Making Strides Against Breast Cancer, the Komen Race for the Cure, or any other women's health–related event.

5

Best Friends
and Bad Hair Days

We may have different beauty methods and
fashion styles, but best friends will never let you
out of the house with bad hair!

If truth is beauty, how come no one has their hair
done in a library?

Lily Tomlin

Whatever happened to those good ol' days when we simply ran a comb through our hair and applied a dash of lipstick? Our beauty regimens used to be much simpler. A hint of mascara, a touch of lipstick, a quick powder of our noses, and we were off.

Now we have to bleach our teeth, make sure our pedicured toes aren't chipped, touch up our French manicures, pluck our unwanted above-the-lip facial hair (also called a "mustache"), "put on our faces," and lather tan-in-a-bottle on any exposed skin before we can set foot out the front door.

My best friend Lana can do all this without batting a mascaraed eyelash—although she hasn't reached the mustache-plucking stage yet—but it takes a little more effort for me.

I usually try to stick to the basics—lipstick, mascara, and a little foundation—but in the summertime I have to do something to my bare legs, especially if I'm "appearing" in public. So for those business engagements where I have to look my professional best, I'll invest in a little bottle tan, courtesy of the drugstore down the street, *and* a salon pedicure.

And the prerequisite mustache plucking.

Most of the time I don't even see my faint mustache. But when the morning sun floods the car and lights up the mir-

66

ror on my sun visor as I'm applying my makeup, there's no escaping the fact.

"I look like a man!" I wail to Michael.

"Look! Look," I'll say when he stops for a red light. "See those little dark hairs on either side of my mouth? Don't tell me you can't *see* them. Oh no, one's half-white and half-brown. Now even my mustache is going gray!"

Michael's in a no-win situation here. No matter what he says, it's going to be wrong.

Lana never lets that stop her.

She'll come over to pick me up for one of our girls' afternoons out, tilt her head to one side, squint at my face, and announce in loving best-friendship, "Your mustache hairs are showing—you need to pluck a couple on your left side."

Or, "Your hair's too flat. You need to pouf it up just a bit."

"I can't. It's too limp. It won't *do* anything today!"

"Here, let me try." And she grabs the brush and hairspray and goes to work. Five minutes later, voila! I'm a new woman, thanks to my stylish friend.

Only a best friend can get away with telling you when you don't look good. Especially when she comes to the rescue. And always lets you know when you're lookin' good as well. "I *love* your new haircut! Is that a new sweater? That's a great color on you."

But in other beauty areas concerning yours truly, Lana's turned in her fashion police badge.

For instance, the last time I had a manicure was on my wedding day. Instead, I have an inexpensive, at-home manicure that I prefer: biting my nails. It's free, it's easy, and I've now perfected a technique of getting them all the same length.

While Lana will get her hair professionally colored or highlighted—and something called "weaved"—at a nice salon every eight weeks, I forego expensive haircuts in favor of my twelve-dollar SuperCuts just three blocks away. I'll also occasionally buy an over-the-counter wash-that-gray-right-outta-my-hair rinse that's good for thirty days.

But there *is* one beauty salon secret that I confess I allow myself to indulge in a few times a year—a professional pedicure. The first time I had one—courtesy of Lana, naturally—I felt luxuriously decadent (and glad I'd shaved my legs the day before). After helping me up the steps to the pedicure throne, the manicurist gently lowered my feet into a miniature hot tub of swirling, bubbling water.

> *Instead, I have an inexpensive, at-home manicure that I prefer: biting my nails.*

Ah . . . ecstasy. But wait—that's only the beginning.

After patting my feet dry, she then rubbed a wonderful oil onto my feet and legs, deeply massaging my legs up to the knees. I felt like a movie star. My feet had never looked—or

68

felt—more beautiful. They were soft and revitalized, with the final pièce de résistance: fire-engine red toes. No way was I going to cover up those beauties with pantyhose. Instead, Lana took me to a nearby department store where she bought me a pretty silver toe ring.

I've long given up the pantyhose ghost. I HATE pantyhose. They're always trying to strangle me. Luckily, I live in California, where bare legs are de rigueur.

Although you couldn't prove it by my mom. "Honey, aren't you going to wear nylons with that nice outfit?" she'll ask.

"No, Mom. Nylons are passé. Don't you ever read *People* magazine? You'll never catch Nicole Kidman or Michelle Pfeiffer in nylons. Their feet are always bare—except for a couple coats of polish on their toes—and they show them off in strappy sandals."

Of course, I'm no movie star. And Nicole's a little younger than me. But Michelle Pfeiffer's about my age, and I never see HER in nylons. Come to think of it, the only Hollywood stars I see in pantyhose are the sixty- or seventy-something ones.

But most Southern women, as Annette reminded me—and probably some from the East Coast, too—wouldn't be caught dead in public without their nylons.

I realized this in Hot Springs, Arkansas, when I spoke at a breast cancer luncheon fund-raiser a couple years ago. Back home in California, I'd felt quite pleased with my wardrobe choice—a well-cut, dressy black pantsuit with a fuchsia silk blouse, a pink enamel breast cancer ribbon pin on my lapel, pretty earrings, my best dress sandals from Payless, and of course, my expensive pedicure.

Until I went into the ladies' room and encountered a seventy-something Southern woman with upswept silver hair, fussing with a beautiful silk scarf at her slender throat. This Southern belle, who was still quite the beauty, was exquisitely attired in a gorgeous camel suit, the aforementioned scarf, chunky gold jewelry, hose, and expensive leather pumps that screamed "Italian."

Definitely a member of the country club set.

I felt a little out of my league and woefully under-dressed.

She was what my Southern friend Sheila would call "high cotton." (Rich and well-connected.)

Next to her, I was a cotton ball.

But as the luncheon continued, I was vindicated. After my talk—which was well-received, despite my somewhat under-dressed appearance—they held an elegant fashion show from an upscale boutique where slacks cost eight hundred dollars a pair and dresses cost more than my car.

At one point, the slim, designer-clad announcer said, "Ladies, you don't have to wear pantyhose anymore!" and stuck out her nylon-free, black-sandaled foot with plum-polished toes for emphasis. "See? Nylons are *out*. But you *must* have a good pedicure," she instructed.

For once I was on the cutting edge of fashion. Lana would have been proud of me as I confidently flashed my fuchsia-painted toes—complete with silver toe ring.

I'm not the only friend who usually sticks out like a fashion sore thumb next to little Lana. There was the time she and Griff, her best friend from college, were at an upscale corporate retreat center in the country one weekend, where Griff, who was working in publicity and media relations, was doing a presentation.

The two friends got up to go running one morning, and Lana was clad in a complete matching jogging outfit and shoes; Griff was in a sweatshirt with the sleeves cut off and raggedy sweatpants.

Griff took one look at Lana and said, "Here's Oscar and Felix out for our morning run."

I'm Oscar to my mom's Felix.

Mom, whose high school yearbook described her as "a charming lass, with ah such class," is a proper and elegant woman from the old school who spends an hour a day curling her hair before she'll venture outside.

When I first began doing radio interviews to promote my books, she'd read somewhere that "you should dress as if you're going to work" to be psychologically prepared for the interview, so she thought I should shower, dress, and put on makeup as if I were going out to work.

What Mom forgot is that my "work clothes" are usually

sweats or a robe. I told her I could be quite psychologically prepared in my Winnie-the-Pooh slippers and favorite fuddy-duddy flannel nightgown.

If I were a high-powered business executive—which, thankfully, I'm not—I'd dress the part in a power suit and pumps. But because I'm a writer and live in northern California, I can get away with a more arty, casual look. I love being able to wear long, flowing print skirts, vests, and boots, or loose-fitting pants and oversized T-shirts.

Especially because for five years in the Air Force, most days I wore my dress blues and pumps. After mustering out and joining the secretarial workforce, I traded in the dress blues for dress pinks, reds, greens, and a variety of other colored business suits and dresses—still with the obligatory pumps.

If I never wear pumps again, that's fine with me. But I do keep a couple pairs in my closet—one black, one navy—for the occasional business or media appearance or winter speaking engagement when open-toed sandals would be too cold.

Some people feel quite strongly about "the proper way to dress." Many set great store on dressing for success and are offended if you don't wear a three-piece suit or a dress, stockings, and pumps to church or a business event. A couple women have even offered to take me under their well-dressed wings and show me the way. Their perfectly-manicured hands are just itching to give me a full head-to-toe makeover.

72

But I think I'll stick to my California girl casual. And just don a dressy blazer and slacks or skirt for the appropriate occasion.

No nylons, though. That's where I draw the line.

Excuse me while I go buy some more tan-in-a-bottle.

> The LORD does not look at the things man looks at. Man looks at the outward appearance, but the LORD looks at the heart.
>
> *1 Samuel 16:7*

Girl Pearls Set up a beauty day and go with a girl-friend to get a manicure or pedicure (trust me, you're going to *love* the latter!). If your pocketbook doesn't allow for a trip to a beauty salon, then set up your own salon at home. Buy some inexpensive nail polish at your local drugstore and take turns painting each other's fingernails and toenails.

6

Chick Flicks, Chatter, and Chocolate

A perfect girl day would include a talky English
film à la *Sense and Sensibility* or a great tearjerker like *Steel Magnolias,* plenty of chocolate,
and lots of chatter afterward
with our girlfriend(s).

Where would we be without the movies?

Nancy Reagan

love movies. Always have. Next to reading, it's my favorite pastime.

Ever since I was a little girl and my folks would let me stay up to watch the late show (no, not Letterman, the late *movie*) on TV with them, I've lost myself in the silver screen. From musicals and westerns to detective yarns and three-hanky dramas, I loved 'em all.

But it was always the "women's" movies—or in my case, "girls'" movies, now commonly known as "chick flicks"—that I most enjoyed. Movies like *Little Women, Sabrina,* or *Marjorie Morningstar* with the beautiful Natalie Wood.

There was another Natalie Wood movie I'll always remember—even though it wasn't one of her big hits (although it did introduce a good-looking newcomer named Robert Redford)—called *Inside Daisy Clover,* about a young girl's ascent to stardom. There was a great song "she" sang (Natalie's voice was dubbed) about getting wings and being eager to fly. That movie, and others like it, showed me there was a big, wide world out there beyond our small Midwestern town—a world I was determined to see.

But before I could grow up and see the world, I had to content myself with movies that allowed me to leave my Wisconsin town in search of more exotic fare. Like *The Moon-*

spinners, Where the Boys Are, A Summer Place, and of course, all the Tammy and Gidget movies I saw on TV.

What prepubescent girl of the '60s could ever forget gorgeous James Darren as Moondoggie singing "Gidget Goes Hawaiian" to the perky Deborah Walley?

But I think the first real, official chick flick I saw in a movie theater was when I was about eleven and my mom took my sister and me to see *Funny Girl,* starring Barbra Streisand. That movie—and Barbra's incredible voice—had a lasting impact on me.

A little more than ten years later when I was stationed in Europe, I found myself on the deck of a ferry going from Dover, England, to Calais, France, at one o'clock in the morning, pretending to be Barbra and belting out "Don't Rain on my Parade" into the heavy mist and choppy early morning waters.

What can I say? I've always had a great fantasy life. Besides, everyone else was inside, and between the roar of the engine and the waves, they couldn't hear a thing.

It wasn't until high school—by this time we'd left Wisconsin for the warmer climate of Arizona—that I was old enough to go to the movies "alone" (with a girlfriend).

And I quickly made up for lost time.

My best friend in high school, Dawn Alexander, and I went to the movies every chance we got—especially on those dateless Saturday nights. Some of our favorite chick flicks of that time included *The Way We Were, What's Up Doc,* and *Alice Doesn't Live Here Anymore.* We were especially fond of musicals, but that was a little tricky, because in the early '70s there weren't too many of those around—which is why we were so thrilled when *Cabaret* came out. We took turns pretending to be Liza Minnelli, belting out song after song. And after our graduation, we had the thrill of visiting Las Vegas with Dawn's family and seeing Liza *live* onstage.

Following the movie, we'd often head to a local coffee shop or Farrell's Ice Cream Parlor, where we'd chatter on about the merits of Robert Redford or Ryan O'Neal over a shared giant hot fudge sundae or rich chocolate cake.

After a good movie, conversation with a good friend, and great chocolate, all's right with the world.

After a good movie, conversation with a good friend, and *great* chocolate, all's right with the world.

When I was stationed in England with the Air Force, my roommate Diane and I would often take the train from Oxford into London together—just to see a movie (of course, we'd also try to fit in an hour or so at the National Gallery or get discounted tickets to a West End play). Fond movie memories include *The Turning Point* with Anne Bancroft—although it was Mikhail Baryshnikov who captured our eyes and hearts—*The Goodbye Girl* with Richard Dreyfuss romancing Marsha Mason on that New York rooftop, and *Ice Castles* with Robby Benson and Lynn Holly Johnson and that great, sappy theme song "Looking Through the Eyes of Love."

It was also in London where we saw the just-released *Grease* with John Travolta and Olivia Newton-John. And for months afterward whenever we had parties at our house, we'd force our guests to watch us lip-sync the songs from the soundtrack— "Summer Lovin'" or "You're the One That I Want—ooh, ooh, ooh, honey!" using the bulky English extension cords with an end that resembled a microphone.

Ah, those were the days.

But one of my favorite movies that we saw together was *New York, New York,* a musical by Martin Scorsese and starring Robert DeNiro—yes, Robert DeNiro—and my pal Liza Minnelli. When Liza sang the show-stopping title number, I got chills. It was one of those magical movie moments. The following year, Frank Sinatra recorded "New York, New York," and it became one of his signature tunes. (So, how many of you knew that Liza sang it before Frank, and in a movie no less?)

That's why I always win at Silver Screen Trivial Pursuit.

Chick flicks bind us together—usually because they're about relationships and talking, and we women love to talk, especially about relationships. As long as there's plenty of chocolate.

My colleague Leona says her favorite chick flick is *Fried Green Tomatoes.*

That's a great girlfriends movie, full of love, loyalty, courage, and standing up for your friends, no matter what the cost. Plus, the women aren't "wimpy"—something my friend Kim hates in a film.

Ditto.

Chick flicks bind us together—usually because they're about relationships and talking.

After so many years of seeing women—most commonly referred to as "the girl"—on the silver screen stand helplessly by and scream during a crisis, while their men were getting beat up, or whatever, it's refreshing to see a strong, smart woman outwit a man and not be afraid to mix it up and get her hands dirty.

I watch that movie at least once a year. And even though it's a chick flick, Michael likes it just as much as I do.

One of the things my friend Joyce likes to do with her four single adult daughters is to take them out to "Chick Flick Daughter Days."

"There's something special about sharing a bulging box of popcorn and drinks," Joyce said. "Recently I took them to see *My Big Fat Greek Wedding.* Although we're Italian, we could really relate to the closeness of a wonderfully loving and boisterous family. We all loved the honesty of this movie

80

because it showed the family to have flaws. We blew our socks off with laughter. It's so wonderful to share this precious time with girls, daughters, and friends."

My friend Jan and her best friend Jeanne love all the old Rodgers and Hammerstein musicals (I do, too), as well as old black-and-white movies that Jan tapes off cable—mostly romantic dramas and a few comedies. "My thrifty friend would never think of paying for cable," said Jan, with a laugh, "but she's thrilled that I do. We forego the chocolate (unless Jeanne is hormonal, and then she always bakes chocolate chip cookies, which I swear I won't eat but always do), but mostly we make tapioca pudding."

Jan and Jeanne have visited England together. "We simply awed our way through the Brontë parsonage and walked the moors behind the authors' childhood home where they lived and died so young," recalled Jan. "We watch all the versions of *Jane Eyre,* but our favorite's the original with Orson Welles."

After visiting Bath—which got its name from the Roman baths made from the natural hot springs there, and which is also where Jane Austen lived—the best friends had a yen to see all Jane Austen's movies, so they rented *Pride and Prejudice* (the A&E version). As much as they love this recent rendition, Jan and Jeanne say they still love the original with Laurence Olivier and Greer Garson.

Later, at a getaway at Jan's little cabin in the woods, the duo hunkered down with two bowls of tapioca "while whimpering through *Sense and Sensibility.*"

Lana and I loved that Jane Austen movie, too. It's a classic chick flick. Beautiful scenery; witty, literate dialogue; sweeping romance; unrequited love; broken hearts; wonderful friendship; and of course, those great English accents. For a brief time afterward, we found ourselves calling each other "Dearest" the way the loving Dashwood sisters—played beautifully in the film by the incomparable Emma Thompson and Kate Winslet—did.

But then, Lana and I always immerse ourselves in the movies we see. We'll leave the theater intently discussing ambiguous endings and what *we* think happened afterward.

"Do you think they stayed together?"

"Definitely. Although, there were probably some struggles. Blah, blah, blah . . ."

"Do you think she followed him?"

"She'd better have! If it were me, I'd have blah, blah, blah . . ."

"Do you think Scarlett got Rhett back?"

"Yes, but I think it took some time. It didn't happen overnight. Blah, blah, blah."

My best friend and I have wrung out many a sodden hanky after watching such favorite weepies as *Out of Africa, Steel Magnolias,* and *Beaches.* But since we also enjoy a good

82

romantic comedy, we also like *Sleepless in Seattle, While You Were Sleeping, You've Got Mail,* and the quintessential single women's movie: *Crossing Delancey* with "the pickle man." If you haven't seen this delightful '80s film with Amy Irving and Peter Riegert about looking beyond the surface, go out and rent it—especially if you're single. You won't be disappointed. And although it's not set in the South, there's even a funny chin-hair plucking scene in it.

Jan says when she and Jeanne are feeling particularly playful, they watch Elvis in *Blue Hawaii.* "We both remember him fondly and always talk about how he was so exploited by Hollywood—forced to waste his talent on those silly musicals," Jan said.

The friends are also nuts over all the *Tammy* movies. "We can sing every line of the Debbie Reynolds song 'Tammy's in Love' with little prompting."

Jan told me this after she and I had just finished watching a wonderful old Susan Hayward movie together up at her cabin—*My Foolish Heart.* As we sniffled together over the ending, we began discussing favorite old chick flicks we loved.

Oldies but Goodies: Three-Hanky Chick Flick Dramas

Random Harvest—Greer Garson and Ronald Colman. I cry *every* time I see this great, enduring love story about a soldier with amnesia and the showgirl who nurtures him back to health. The fact that it's set in England doesn't hurt either.

Dark Victory—Bette Davis dying of a brain tumor and falling in love with her doctor, George Brent. (Humphrey Bogart and a young Ronald Reagan are also featured.)

Now, Voyager—Bette Davis and Paul Henreid. ("Don't let's ask for the moon, Jerry. We've got the stars!")

Kitty Foyle—Ginger Rogers. No dancing and no Fred, but Ginger won an Oscar for her dramatic performance in this 1940 "soap opera" about the troubled love life of a secretary from the wrong side of the tracks.

A Guy Named Joe—Spencer Tracy and Irene Dunne. Steven Spielberg's *Always* with Richard Dreyfuss and Holly Hunter is a remake of this classic tearjerker.

The Best Years of Our Lives—Fredric March, Myrna Loy, Teresa Wright, and Dana Andrews. American soldiers returning home after World War II to the women they left behind. A real-life serviceman, Harold Russell, who lost both arms below the elbow in the war, delivers a moving supporting performance—for which he won an Oscar.

Somewhere in Time—Jane Seymour and Christopher Reeve. Okay, I know this isn't that old—1980—but it has a gentle, old-fashioned feel to it. This tender love story with a twist requires copious amounts of tissues.

And of course, the top three classic romantic drama chick flicks of all time:

An Affair to Remember—Cary Grant and Deborah Kerr. ("Oh darling, don't worry, darling! If you can paint, I can walk!") For those of you under thirty who've never seen it, this was the classic love story featured in *Sleepless in Seattle* about the couple who's to reconnect on top of the Empire State Building, only she never shows—for a very good reason. A chick flick MUST.

Gone with the Wind—Clark Gable and Vivien Leigh. Need I say more?

Casablanca—Ingrid Bergman and Humphrey Bogart. My favorite movie of all time, with the best—and most-quoted—lines ever. "I think this is the beginning of a beautiful friendship . . ."

Although *The African Queen* is an adventure rather than a romantic comedy or three-hanky drama, the improbable love story between the prim spinster missionary Rose (Katharine Hepburn) and the crusty, unwashed good-time Charlie (Humphrey Bogart) is in a romantic chick flick class all its own.

"Classic" (old) Chick Flick Romantic Comedies

It Happened One Night—This Clark Gable–Claudette Colbert delight won a bunch of Academy Awards. Newspaperman Clark teaching spoiled runaway heiress Claudette the proper way to dunk a doughnut is priceless. So is the hitchhiking scene.

The Philadelphia Story—Cary Grant, Katharine Hepburn, and Jimmy Stewart. Need I say more?

Holiday—The wonderful Cary Grant and Katharine Hepburn yet again.

Adam's Rib, Woman of the Year, and *Desk Set.* The battle of the sexes has never been fought better—and funnier—than with Spencer Tracy and Katharine Hepburn.

Roman Holiday—Gorgeous Gregory Peck, and introducing the incomparable Audrey Hepburn.

Sabrina—Audrey Hepburn, Humphrey Bogart, and a blond William Holden.

Born Yesterday—Judy Holliday and William Holden. The brassy blond gets a crash course in culture from William Holden and turns out to not be so dumb after all.

To Catch a Thief—Cary Grant and Grace Kelly directed by Alfred Hitchcock. Talk about fireworks.

And . . . all those Doris Day favorites from the '50s and

86

early '60s: *Pillow Talk, Teacher's Pet, Please Don't Eat the Daisies,* and *That Touch of Mink.*

Since Jan and I are both rabid Anglophiles, we're partial to talky English films—as are most of my girlfriends.

Great Talky English Chick Flicks

A Room with a View—Helena Bonham Carter, Julian Sands and THAT KISS in Italy. (Also features the wonderful Maggie Smith and Judi Dench before she was a Dame of the British Empire.)

Enchanted April—Four English women of varying ages and backgrounds become friends while spending some memorable girl time in Italy.

84 Charing Cross Road—Anthony Hopkins and Anne Bancroft as book lovers and transatlantic pen pals.

Truly, Madly, Deeply—Juliet Stevenson grieving a lost love (Alan Rickman) but then letting go and moving on.

Emma, Persuasion, and *Mansfield Park*—a Jane Austen triple threat.

Much Ado About Nothing—Shakespeare brought wonderfully to life by Kenneth Branagh and Emma Thompson.

Tea with Mussolini—the formidable Maggie Smith, Joan

Plowright, Dame Judi Dench, and Cher. Yes, Cher. Fabulous.

An Ideal Husband—Jeremy Northam, Cate Blanchett, Rupert Everett, Minnie Driver, and Julianne Moore. An ideal cast and an ideal movie.

And of course, the best of the best, the aforementioned *Sense and Sensibility* with Emma Thompson, Hugh Grant, Alan Rickman, and Kate Winslet.

Movies made from Jane Austen's novels are a favorite with many women.

My twenty-something colleague Heather also enjoys A&E's *Pride and Prejudice.* "It's five hours long and can't be watched without several good girlfriends and a pint of Ben & Jerry's," she said.

But of all my girlfriends—all of them like going to the movies—the most enthusiastic film-buff friend in my life is Lonnie. Films are as much a passion to her as they are to me, and we're *always* talking about them. The only problem is . . . she lives in Michigan and I live in California. So we've only been to a couple movies together.

Once when she came out for a visit, I took her to our local art-house theater to see the amazing *Crouching Tiger, Hidden Dragon,* which hadn't yet opened in Michigan—not your typical chick flick, I know. (Who'd ever think martial arts and

88

romance could meld so well together?) Although I'd already seen the movie, I loved it just as much the second time. Maybe even more so as I listened to my friend's delighted gasps and enraptured sighs next to me.

A few months later, Lonnie recommended *My Big Fat Greek Wedding* to me—while it was still playing in obscure art-house theaters and before it became the romantic comedy megahit of 2002. Lonnie's half Greek, so of course, before I saw it I thought that might be why she loved it so much. But when I watched it, I realized it was because it was so true-to-life for EVERY family, no matter what ethnic background. It was fresh, real, and screamingly hilarious.

Recently, my film-buff friend and I were talking about some new movies we were simply dying to see—wishing it could be somehow together—and she said plaintively, "Maybe we could meet in Kansas?"

Lonnie's such a cinemaphile that for her fiftieth birthday party, she rented her favorite old movie theater in the small Michigan town where she'd grown up and showed Alfred Hitchcock's *North by Northwest* to 150 of her friends and family. Since we couldn't be there, Michael and I bought her the DVD as a birthday present and overnighted it to her for the party. Then, my sweet, sentimental husband, who also loves my friend, went out and bought a copy of the same DVD for us.

And the day of the party, we snuggled in with the same

movie—at 2:30 Michigan time, 11:30 California time—and raised our glasses in a birthday toast across the miles to my movie-loving friend.

Here's lookin' at you, kid.

> If there's a way of saying "I love you" without saying it—that's film.
>
> *Buster Keaton*

Girl Pearls   Go on a girls' night out to the movies. Or have a movie day at home, with lots of popcorn and chocolate, and rent three or four of your favorite misty-eyed chick flicks. Not in the mood for a good cry? Watch a couple of these delightful romantic comedies instead: *When Harry Met Sally, The Princess Bride, Murphy's Romance, Notting Hill,* and one of my all-time favorite romantic comedies, *The Parent Trap* with Hayley Mills. Yes, it's ROMANTIC. Trust me. Rent it again and you'll see what I mean.

7

Cat Women versus Dog Women

Just what is it with women and their cats?
I'm a dog woman all the way.
Girlfriends and their pets.

Some of our greatest historical and artistic treasures
we place in museums; others we take for walks.

Roger A. Caras

've never been a cat woman. Or a dog woman either, for that matter.

When all my single women friends were getting cats, I was never once tempted to become a kitty mama. It seemed like some unspoken rite of passage to me—if you were a single woman over thirty, you had to own at least one cat.

I'll never forget one brilliant reporter I worked with years ago when I was just starting out in the newspaper business. She was incredibly smart, well-read, and somewhat cynical, with a biting, caustic wit. I was a little intimidated by her.

The one thing I'd never have pegged her for was soft or sentimental.

Then I stopped by her apartment one day to pick her up for a movie, and I saw a totally different woman. A mushy, gushy, woman when it came to her cats . . . "Where's mommy's 'ittle girl? Are you hiding? Come to mama. That's a good girl . . ."

But this hard-bitten reporter-turned-to-mush over a little ball of fur had *nothing* on my girlfriend Karen, who is the proud parent of three cats: Naomi, Mister, and Anna.

Karen hasn't always been so cat-inclined.

On her fifth birthday she received her first kitten. "I remember hugging it to my chest as I ran next door to trade it

92

for a puppy," she recalled. "My parents were not amused. I announced emphatically, 'I hate cats! I like puppies.'"

Now she refers to her three cats as "purr puppies."

"I have always been a dog person," Karen says. "Until one day, ten years ago, a stray cat walked out of the rain and into my house and heart. I fed it and then picked it up—only to be clawed. I still have the scar, and the cat.

"I told the cat, 'I am an intense person who takes being a "pet parent" seriously,'" Karen said. "I named the cat Naomi and mumbled something about 'Where you go I go. Your people will be my people, and only death will separate us.'"

Naomi moved with Karen from a lovely house in the San Francisco Bay Area across the country to a small, one-bedroom New York City apartment that they shared with a roommate, Stephanie, a film and stage actress who was highly allergic to cats, so she lived on Claritin.

Whenever Karen had to leave town on business, she'd call home and ask her roommate if she could speak to Naomi. A good roommate and a good girlfriend, Stephanie complied, but she warned Karen, "If you ever tell anyone I put a cat on the phone, I'll deny it." Once when Karen called, Stephanie informed her friend, "Naomi can't come to the phone, we're playing Monopoly and she's the banker. Got to run, she just bought Park Place," and hung up.

Every time Karen called, Stephanie, the consummate actress, would yell out comments like, "Naomi, you're not leaving here dressed like *that,* missy!" or "Naomi, *way* too much rouge," or, "Naomi, you'll break your neck in those heels."

Good thing Stephanie's allergic to cats. Otherwise, she and Naomi would have been painting the town red every night.

One day during Karen's first year in New York, she decided that Naomi needed some fresh air, so she bought a leash and took her to Central Park. "We were across the street from the Plaza Hotel when I placed her down on the sidewalk," Karen recalled. "I proceeded to walk Naomi behind me; or so I thought. People were staring at me, but I assumed it was because they were walking Dobermans or German shepherds and *I* was walking a gray tabby cat.

"Until I looked around to see Naomi lying limp on her side. By all appearances, I was dragging a dead cat behind me."

When Naomi and Karen moved from New York back to California (Sacramento, this time), Naomi got sick. "She had a rash and was lethargic," Karen recalled. "The vet said, 'Allergy'; I said, 'She needs a playmate.' But Naomi had neglected to inform Karen that all purr puppies are not alike. Or she'd never have brought home the "evil twins." "Anna and Mister looked identical to my Princess Naomi. They're gray tabbies, but they act like the two Siamese cats from *Lady and the Tramp.*"

Karen, a former actress, does voices for each of her cats.

"Naomi has beautiful, big eyes, so her voice is that of a Brooklyn Jewish mother," said Karen. "Mister Man's eyes look

94

as if he is not quite sure where he is or how he got there, so my voice for him is that of Lenny in *Of Mice and Men*. Anna's eyes are small, piercing, look-straight-through-you eyes that say, 'I know everything about you and I'm going to tell.' Her voice is that of a soft-spoken British lady. Anna is constantly saying, 'Am I pretty, mummy?'" Karen related in a dead-on English accent.

Anna is very smart, says her proud purr-puppy mom. "She is the only one of my three cats who has not caught herself on fire."

Karen enjoys having candles burning around the house. But one night, Naomi walked over to a lighted candle, caught her stomach on fire, and didn't even know it. "I chased her through the house screaming, 'Drop and roll! Drop and roll!'" Karen recalled. Naomi ran under the bed, snuffing out the flames.

And Mister Man once caught his tail on fire.

Karen smelled fur burning as Mister Man casually walked through the living room, so she threw herself on top of him and patted his tail end until he was flame free.

Mister weighs twenty-two pounds and is afraid of everyone except Karen and his nanny.

"Yes, I have a cat nanny," Karen admitted.

"When I go out of town on business, Nanny Jillian comes to take care of them. Nanny Jillian calls me once a day so I can speak with each cat. Once, Jillian called me all upset: "I am so sorry . . . I don't know how they got in your closet," Karen recalled.

"I said, 'You mean Beelzebub and his twin sister Lucy?'"

Jillian had found Anna and Mister swinging from dress to blouse to jacket inside Karen's closet.

> *"God said when he saves us, we're new creations," Karen said. "I believe it. The me prior to Jesus hated cats. Now I cannot imagine my life without them."*

"I told her it was okay. I know how they get in there. I've watched them do it," Karen said. "Anna hangs full-body stretch from the closet door knob, and then Mister Man runs and pushes her. The door knob pops, and in they go."

When Karen goes to sleep alone each night, she wakes every morning to Mister Man lying across her feet, Anna lying on her stomach, and Naomi lying next to her head. "God said when he saves us, we're new creations," Karen said. "I believe it. The me prior to Jesus hated cats. Now I cannot imagine my life without them."

Some of Karen's favorite girl time is spent with Anna and Naomi (but they let Mister Man in on the fun, too.)

Ditto for my friend Lonnie who has two adorable felines named Kit-Kat (a tortoiseshell) and Lucy (a Russian blue). "They're my girls," Lonnie said. "I'm convinced that they're barometers for how I feel."

One day Lonnie tripped and fell down the steep stairs in her old house. She was terrified her lumbar disk was going to bulge—she has a problem from a previous accident—and she had to fly the next day. So she took ibuprofen and crawled into bed, lying on her side.

"The next thing I knew," she recalled, "Kit-Kat—who weighs fifteen pounds—had sprawled across my thigh, and her weight was pulling onto my lower back. Usually she sits on my hip. However, this felt very comfortable. It felt like traction." After a while, Kit-Kat got down and Lonnie turned over. The other cat, Lucy, who weighs twelve pounds, jumped up onto my friend's other thigh and did the same thing.

"I became convinced that they sensed something was wrong and they were somehow able to help," Lonnie says. Amazingly, she had no ill effects from the fall.

When Lucy first came to Lonnie and Joe, the couple tried to find her a home because they didn't think Kit-Kat would get along with her. "Kit-Kat has the strongest personality of anyone in the house," Lonnie says, "and it's sometimes a problem with two female cats. But we got advice from a lot of experts and pet owners who all said to put them together starting just a few minutes at a time, then hours at a time, etc."

The couple followed this advice and kept putting the two cats together over about a ten-day period.

"Finally, we came home one day and Kit-Kat was curled

around Lucy, bathing her," Lonnie said. "Kit-Kat looked up at us as if to say, 'Hey, thanks. I was so lonely. I've got a friend now,' and then went back to grooming Lucy. They've been best girlfriends ever since."

My friend Marian's another cat-loving woman. She's the proud owner of Nessie and Angus McKitty. Here, then, is the tale of Nessie the Neurotic and her adventures in pharmacopoeia.

A year after Marian got Nessie, a beautiful silver tabby, she moved to an apartment on her own, where she had to leave her cat alone while she worked all day.

Nessie didn't appreciate this. In fact, she grew so neurotic that she chewed all the hair off her tail.

"She looked like a silver tabby rat. Or maybe a possum," Marian said.

Concerned, she took her beloved feline to the vet, who tried behavior modification and different drugs. Including Valium.

When Marian brought Nessie home, she followed the directions on the prescription and gave Nessie the required dose. Five minutes later, she heard a strange noise. Going into the kitchen, she saw that Nessie had climbed into her food bowl. As Marian watched, Nessie suddenly fell over backward and then began making her unsteady way down the hall, stumbling like a drunk.

98

Worried, Marian picked up her tabby. "It was like picking up a sandbag," she recalled. "She had no muscle tone and was like Jell-O in my arms." Hysterical, Marian called the vet and cried, "I've ODed my cat!"

While Marian talked to the vet, Nessie slid over her arm and poured herself onto the floor, then began doing an "Esther Williams thing—pushing herself backward in a circle," Marian said.

"What should I do?" my worried friend asked the vet.

"Is she chewing her tail?"

"No."

"Well, then."

Unfortunately, the Valium only lasted about an hour, and soon Nessie was back to chomping on her tail again. After trying various other remedies, the vet suggested that Marian get another cat to keep poor Nessie company.

So one day Marian came home with Angus, a Maine coon, or as she calls him, "klutz cat extraordinaire, always bumping into things, and with a penchant for chewing and breaking things."

One night when Marian came home from work, her apartment manager, who lived below her, asked, "Do you have kids?"

"No."

"Well, all day long I hear this strange thumping sound in your apartment," the manager said.

At first Marian was mystified. What could the noise be? Then she figured it out: Angus.

"He's not smart enough to open the kitchen cupboard doors all at once," Marian said, "so he opens the door a little bit with his paw, and then it closes (thump). Then he tries again, and it closes again (thump), and then again (thump), until finally he gets the door open wide enough so he can slip inside. He's always going into the pots and pans cupboard and making a racket."

Although Marian is a cat woman, she used to be a dog woman.

"Susie was my dog who died the spring before I moved back to Sacramento," Marian said. "She was wonderful. However, I only have one picture of her because every time I got the camera out, she would cower and act as if I were going to beat her! She was blond with short hair, but her eyes were unique because she was a mix of some different breeds. Her eyes were half-blue and half-brown. The skin around her eyes was black, so she looked like she was wearing eyeliner.

"Susie would confess whenever she did anything wrong," Marian recalled. "If I went next door to visit my neighbor, I didn't have to worry about what Susie would do; she would tell me as soon as I walked in the door. Once, she met me at the back door looking 'hangdog' (pun intended). I said gently, 'Susie, what did you do?' She turned and stared sadly at the couch because she knew she wasn't supposed to be on

100

it, but sure enough, there was Susie hair all over it. She also confessed to eating the cat food and pulling leftovers off the kitchen counter."

Denise, Marian's neighbor and best friend, is the happy owner of two dogs: Kendra, a sheltie, and Cookie, a miniature springer spaniel–Border collie mix.

Denise loves her dogs, who are really her kids.

"Kendra's a tattletale," said Denise. "She knows when Cookie's doing something she shouldn't. Just like kids have special cries, dogs have special barks. When she barks a certain way, I know that Cookie's up to something. And sure enough, when I investigate, there's Cookie getting into the garbage."

Kendra also has a special squeaky little greeting she reserves just for Ingrid, her dog-sitter, when Denise is out of town.

We've used the wonderful Ingrid as a dog-sitter, too. We hired her to watch Gracie when we went to England a couple years ago, and asked her to come over a couple days early so we could introduce them to each other.

After meeting, and liking—and licking—Ingrid, Gracie headed back to her normal post by the front window, standing on her hind legs to look out. Suddenly, and without warning, she emitted a little "toot." We'd never seen, or heard, this from our regal Princess Grace Elizabeth before.

Apparently, neither had Gracie.

She got a bewildered look in her eyes and looked around and then at her tail to find the source of the noise. *Where'd that come from?* her expression seemed to say.

Dogs are creatures of routine.

Every morning when we wake up and make our morning tea (we're not coffee drinkers), we'll turn around to see Gracie lying on the rug just outside the kitchen door, looking up at us plaintively.

"What? Do you want your breakfast 'bikkie' (dog biscuit)?" one of us will ask, heading over to the cupboard where we keep her dog treats. By the time we turn around, biscuit in hand, Gracie has disappeared. She likes to "hunt" for her food, so we have to throw the bikkie across the floor so that it lands just outside the kitchen door in the dining room.

From her "den" beneath the dining room table, Gracie dashes to the doorway and pounces on the bikkie—hopefully before it stops moving. Then she scampers back to her den to enjoy her morning snack.

We repeat this ritual three or four times each morning. Gracie likes to play us off each other, so she'll usually demand her breakfast from Michael first. Then when he's in the shower and I'm in the kitchen making his lunch, Gracie will appear at the door with that pitiful look in her eyes, saying, "I'm hungry, Mother." (Yes, she speaks to us.)

Once Michael's gone off to work, Gracie happily settles

into her perch on the chair by the front window, where she can see all the comings and goings of the neighborhood.

And I head to my office to write for the day. I'll be right in the middle of composing a chapter—like now—when without fail, about 8:30 every morning, I'll hear a little noise behind me. I swivel around in my chair, and there's Gracie up on her hind legs, front legs furiously pawing the air, saying, "Please, Mother, it's time for my morning backyard sniff." Sometimes, especially if I'm in the middle of a brilliant sentence I want to finish or a thought I need to get down before I forget (the latter happens more often than the former), I'll say, "Not now, Gracie. In a minute. Mommy's busy."

She'll wait for a couple seconds, and then I'll hear a loud whooshing sound behind me. Gracie's now pawing at the air even faster and throwing in some cute little hops to demonstrate her excitement. If that doesn't work, she'll crawl beneath my desk, lick my pantyhose-free legs, then insinuate her head up into my lap where I can see her, directly beneath my typing fingers.

I glance down, and there's this adorable little white furry face with big dark, soulful eyes staring up at me. What mom can resist?

Michael and I have decided Gracie must be part cat.

She always likes to perch in the highest part of the room. She often lies, not on the chair cushion, but astride the arm of the chair. She even likes to lie on the back of the couch, head on our shoulders, or nose nuzzling our ears.

So naturally, when it's "night-night" time, she heads straight for the pillow. On Michael's side of the bed. Then when he comes into the room, she ignores him or looks up as if to say, "What's HE doing here?" Sometimes, she insists on her pillow throne and stays there even when Michael crawls into bed.

It's quite a sweet picture, dark-haired Michael with his pretty white-fur dog "hat"—that makes me think of Dr. Zhivago—and Gracie, determined not to budge.

But one of my favorite routines Gracie does occurs when I come home—from a ten-minute errand, an afternoon out, or a weeklong trip. It doesn't matter *how* long I'm gone, she reacts the same way.

The minute I walk through the front door, she races to my side, her entire body quivering with relief and delight, and begs frantically for me to pick her up, using her front-paws-whooshing-the-air routine while she hops on her hind legs. "Mommy, Mommy, you've come *home!* You didn't leave me *after* all! I *missed* you!" Whether I've got my hands full with mail, groceries, or suitcases, it doesn't matter. Gracie will keep pestering me until I reach down, pick her up, and give her a big hug.

Sometimes, she barely waits for me to bend down before jumping into my arms all a-quiver, snuggling against my chest and neck and giving me happy doggie kisses.

104

My feline-loving girlfriends can keep their cats. My heart belongs to Gracie.

She's my sweetest girlfriend.

Dog's lives are too short . . . their only fault really.

Agnes Sligh Turnbull

Girl Pearls   Whether you're a dog woman or a cat woman, make sure you carve out plenty of girl time to play with your beloved pets. Whether it's taking them for a good long walk, playing tug-of-war with their favorite chew toy, or rubbing their tummies, stroking their ears, or brushing their fur, they'll appreciate it and, in return, give you their lifelong devotion. (At least dogs will.)

8

Wishin' and Hopin' and Prayin' and Cryin'

A look at those fun single days when we were wishin' and hopin' and prayin' for a relationship with Mr. Right and had to dissect with our girlfriends every pause and nuance of his conversations.

Laugh and the world laughs with you.
Cry and you cry with your girlfriends.

Laurie Kyslansky

o, what did he say then?"

"He asked me if I liked ice cream and wanted to go out after singles group tonight and have some Ben & Jerry's."

"No! Really?"

"Really," I said with shining eyes and great anticipation.

"So he asked you out on a date!"

"D'ya think? Maybe he just likes ice cream . . ."

"Did he ask anyone else to join you?"

"No . . ."

"Well, then it's a date! Call me afterward and tell me *every*thing!"

Turns out it wasn't a date after all—he was just in the mood to go get some ice cream with a friend. Heavy sigh.

Another dating hope bites the dust.

How well I remember those wishin' and hopin' and prayin'-to-meet-Mr.-Right days of singleness. Many were the times those hopes, wishes, and prayers ended up in tears—for me and my single girlfriends.

"But I thought he *liked* me! If he didn't like me, then why'd he hold my hand at the movies and kiss me when he took me home?"

"'Cause he's a guy."

"But if it didn't *mean* anything to him, then why'd he do it?"

"Hormones."

"But you'd think a Christian guy would know better!"

"He's still a guy with hormones."

Being single and a Christian was a confusing business. We wanted to honor God and seek him first and not make meeting Mr. Right our focus. Yet we heard sermons all the time about the joys of marriage, and we were surrounded on all sides by blissfully married couples.

And you know what? *We* had hormones, too. So it was a struggle.

It didn't help when the guys sent us mixed signals.

"You never really knew if it was a date," my best friend Lana recalled of our time together in a large church singles group. "You weren't sure when a guy invited you to do something if he was interested in you or just doing the group-fun thing."

Several of us women in our early thirties decided that the existing single guys at church must have gone through some secret initiation. We figured anytime a new single guy came to the group, the other guys would quickly pull him into the men's room and warn him, "Now, don't sit next to a single woman in church unless you're in a big group, or she'll think you want to marry her. And never, *ever* ask her to do something one-on-one, or she'll start planning the wedding."

Can you say a little over the top? We usually didn't start

planning the wedding until the guy sat next to us at least *twice* in church.

My friend Chuck sat next to me in church all the time, so he shouldn't have been surprised. For three years I was not-so-secretly crazy about the tall, good-looking Chuck, whom I'd met at singles group and become good friends with. I was absolutely *convinced* that Chuck was THE MAN GOD HAD CHOSEN FOR ME (see the "A Norwegian from Wisconsin?" chapter in *Love Handles for the Romantically Impaired*), only he didn't know it yet. So I was willing to be patient until he saw the light.

He never saw the light.

And I made myself alternately crazy and miserable over our "relationship," or lack thereof. It was never more than a friendship on Chuck's part, and he told me that—countless times. But when he'd smile down at me from his tall Norwegian bachelor position and ask me to do something, no matter what my head said—*It doesn't mean anything. He's just a friend. He's not interested in you that way.*—my heart, which is a pretty strong muscle all its own, would always flutter and hope *maybe this time he'll fall . . .*

Lana and I, who were roommates at the time, would have long talks about Chuck—who was also her friend—and my feelings for him. Although she liked and respected him, I was her best friend and she didn't want to see me get hurt. So finally the day came when my wise and practical friend gently

110

but firmly said to me, "Laura, you need to stop spending so much time with Chuck. You know he only wants to be friends, but you want more, and being around him all the time is setting yourself up for heartache and disappointment."

I acknowledged that she was right and agreed to move on and stop doing things with the Chuck-man of my dreams.

A few days after this heartfelt conversation, Lana went on a daylong singles event—which I'd declined to attend, pleading too much homework (which was true). But later that day, Chuck called and asked me to go out to a matinee with him and another friend.

Guess what I did?

Movie lover that I am, I couldn't refuse. It had nothing to do with Chuck.

At least that's what I told Lana when she called a little later, on the way home from her outing, to invite me to pizza with the gang.

I don't understand why she got angry. She was leading with her head; I was leading with my masochistic heart.

Thankfully, after three years Chuck moved to Texas, and I finally realized that there was something to that old cliché "Out of sight, out of mind." Not wanting to waste any more time pining away after someone I couldn't have, for my thirty-fourth birthday I took out a personal ad in the *Pennysaver* that said, "Wanted: A Christian man who reads!"

Only problem: I forgot to read the fine print that said

every time I called the 900 number to listen to the responses to my ad, I was charged thousands and thousands of pennies.

I took out a personal ad in the Pennysaver that said, "Wanted: A Christian man who reads!"

When my phone bill arrived a few weeks later with more than four hundred dollars in charges, I hung up my man-hunting hat. It cost too much. That's when I decided to let God do the hunting for me.

Since my wishin' and hopin' singles days are now in the distant past, I thought I'd better talk to some of today's single women—to see how much things have changed.

Not much.

My twenty-four-year-old niece Kari, whom you met earlier, is a hopeless romantic, just like I was.

"Anytime a guy calls, I save the message," Kari said, "then I'll call my sister Jennie, and say, 'Listen to this message! Does this sound like he likes me?'"

Kari and Jennie have played the wishin' and hopin' game together since they were teens.

"Guess what? That new guy in Sunday school smiled at me this morning!"

"He did? I *told* you he liked you!"

"You'll never believe what happened! I bumped into that cute guy from English today on my way to class."

"You did? Did he ask for your phone number?"

"No, but he touched my arm when he said, 'Excuse me.'"

A few years after high school, things took a more serious turn when Jennie began dating a coworker, Jason.

"I realized how much he cared for Jennie when she had to tell him about her past and some of the consequences of it," Kari recalled. "The very next day Jason wrote her a sweet, beautiful poem that basically said the past was the past and it didn't change his feelings for her. That's when I knew she was gonna marry this guy . . ."

Shortly after Jason gave Jennie the poem, when things were starting to get more serious between them—and before Kari had even met him—Jennie was talking to Jason on the phone one night and suddenly began bawling. "Then she handed me the phone and said *I* had to talk to him because she couldn't," Kari recalled. "I'd never talked to him before then, and he was wondering what was wrong with Jennie, why she was crying.

"So I told him, 'She doesn't feel that she deserves you, Jason. She's never felt this way before; she's never pictured herself being a wife and mother, and what scares her is that she *can* picture that with you, and she's wondering why you'd pick her out of all the women you could have.'"

In the background, Kari could hear Jennie say through her gulping sobs, "Oh yes . . . that's it . . ."

What a touching twinship connection—one sister speaking for the other.

My colleague Leona is thankful that her girlfriend Dawn had the guts to speak up and be completely honest with her when she was in a bad relationship.

"I was trying to break it off, slowly, but was still hanging on a lot emotionally," Leona recalled. "She helped me see the negative spots where 'love was blind,' and it gave me the courage to walk away for good. When I think about this now, and how incredible my husband is, I'm so grateful for honest friends!"

Heather, a single colleague, said, "My friends and I talk about guys all the time. One of my friends called me this summer at 4:00 A.M. because she had just found out her ex-boyfriend was dating someone else. We live in separate states and hardly see each other, but whenever I have guy trouble, she's the first one I call."

Girlfriends are a big help in the guy area.

Take my friend Marya.

"We four girls lived in a campus apartment, and none of us had any boyfriends—a fact over which we commiserated often, usually with bowls overflowing with ice cream," Marya recalled. "So when I came home one day to news that I'd

114

received a call from A BOY, my roommates twittered with questions. The 'boy,' a man I'd met at church, had gotten my number from the church directory and thought I might like to see a play with him. At least that was the stated reason for his call.

"My roommates were certain it had to mean so much more."

When the blessed night arrived, Marya worried under her excitement that she was about to cross into "a place of no return."

"The four of us had been a team for months, free of the dynamic of a man in our midst," she recalled. "My fear of 'breaking ranks' soon disappeared, however, in a way I will never forget.

"Near the time my date was to arrive, it was discovered that my full-length wool coat was covered with—gasp—annoying flecks of lint. Of course, this would never do, and trekking into the December night without it was not an option. I was lost for ideas, but each of my roommates went to task on my behalf," Marya said. "They ganged up on the offending garment with Scotch tape wrapped in reverse around their hands. With double-fisted fury, my three roommates attacked the fuzz and rendered my coat wearable.

"That date and that man have long since passed from my life," Marya said, "but I snapped a photo that night of those incredibly unselfish women. I will never forget what they did for me that day."

None of us can forget our girlfriends who generously lend an ear, a tissue, or even some Scotch tape during our wishin' and hopin' and prayin' and cryin' days.

Let's hear it for the girls!

> I have learned that to have a good friend is the purest of all God's gifts, for it is a love that has no exchange of payment.

Frances Farmer

Girl Pearls Whether you're married or wishin' and hopin' to be married, for fun gather together a group of your girlfriends to play board games one night. (For sheer, goofy silliness, round up someone's old Mystery Date game and see which dream date you wind up with now, and how your tastes have changed since childhood.)

9

Wedding Wonder Women

Our girlfriends who stand up for us on this
most important day—and those who work
behind the scenes—help make our special day
a wedding to remember.
They're deserving of honor.

Love is kind and patient, never jealous, boastful, proud,
or rude. Love isn't selfish or quick tempered. . . . Love is always
supportive, loyal, hopeful, and trusting.

1 Corinthians 13:4, 7 CEV

W hen my sister-in-law Sheri got married in a simple ceremony more than twenty-five years ago, her sister Debbie was the matron of honor and was an absolute godsend to Sheri.

"She sewed her matron of honor dress *and* her daughter's flower girl dress, she single-handedly made the wedding cake and brought it up to Sacramento from San Jose (where she was living), and she helped with the wedding breakfast," Sheri remembered. "She did *every*thing, orchestrated *every*thing. I didn't feel like I had to do anything on my wedding day other than show up and put on my dress. Debbie was not at all concerned about herself on my special day, her focus was on me—it wasn't about her at all."

Which is as it should be.

A woman's wedding day is one of the happiest—and often, most stressful—days of her life. And good friends—especially maids or matrons of honor—can go a long way toward reducing the bride's stress and making it a day to remember.

Twenty-three years after Debbie helped make Sheri's wedding special, Sheri's daughter Kari did the same thing for her twin sister, Jennie.

Kari, Jennie's maid of honor, accompanied her twin to all her fittings; helped pick out the songs, her colors, and the

118

flowers; and in general, acted like a wedding coordinator for the happy event.

"Jennie wasn't at all stressed on her wedding day," Kari recalled. "I was."

Kari also bought the toasting flutes and glasses for all the bridesmaids and groomsmen, the wedding favors, and the "something new" for her sister to wear—the beautiful tiara headpiece that made Jennie look, and feel, like a princess.

The wedding was lovely and touching, particularly when Jennie and Jason said their vows. The female guests teared up at the loving emphasis with which Jason underscored every promise to Jennie, eyes only on his beloved.

But there was still more emotion to come at the reception.

Kari knew that as maid of honor she was expected to offer a toast to the bride and groom, and she wanted it to be something really meaningful for her sister, but she struggled with the words.

"I started working on this the day she asked me to be her maid of honor," Kari recalled, "but I'm not much of a writer. I tried to write something special but couldn't. And then the week before the wedding, I heard the Faith Hill song from *Pearl Harbor,* "There You'll Be," and it was perfect. The lyrics said it better than I could ever write—about how I feel about Jennie, how she was always there for me."

Jennie remembers it well.

"I'd promised myself I wouldn't cry during my wedding ceremony or at the reception," she said, "but then when it came time for Kari to make her toast and she said, 'Jennie, I wanted to do something special for you, but I just didn't know what to say. But there's this song . . . ,' and then I heard the first words of "There You'll Be" and began to cry. I was so overwhelmed because Kari never tells me how much I mean to her, I just know. So for her to do that was completely un-expected and very touching." Jennie said. "There were even guests crying with us."

I can vouch for that since I was one of those guests.

My work friend Leona's sister was also her maid of honor, but she extended her wedding wonder-woman duties beyond the day of the celebration.

"When my husband and I returned from our honeymoon, we entered our 'home' (temporary because we were moving out of state) and found several surprises," Leona recalled. "Lue Ann had a big poster in the kitchen where we first walked in that said, 'Welcome Home, Newlyweds!' She'd stocked the fridge with food, and on the bed she'd put a TV tray with a box of pancake mix, some cereal, syrup, and a note that said 'Breakfast in Bed.'"

"We gave Lue a surprise the next morning, too, when she came over to finish decorating and realized we'd come home early," Leona remembered with a laugh.

120

Lue Ann also brought pictures from the cameras at the reception, already developed. "AND she made a beautiful Creative Memories album with pictures beginning with our wedding showers all the way up to the reception clean-up—which of course, we weren't there for. What a lot of work!" Leona said. "I love it even more than my 'professional' album."

Several wonderful women contributed to make my wedding a memorable occasion—from the beautiful showers that Pat, Lana, Carol, and Sheri threw me, to the gorgeous crystal heart cake topper that my new sister-in-law Debbie gave us.

Knowing that we were pulling our wedding together on a shoestring budget and needing to spend as little money as possible, everyone pitched in to help.

Chris, one of my bridesmaids, who had a special flair for flower arranging, knew we couldn't afford a professional florist, so she suggested we use dried flowers instead. For months in advance she and several other friends and family members cut the best roses from their yards—and the yards of generous neighbors—and hung them upside down

> *Knowing that we were pulling our wedding together on a shoestring budget and needing to spend as little money as possible, everyone pitched in to help.*

to dry in preparation for the wedding. She and her team of helpers later fashioned the flowers into beautiful bouquets, corsages, and boutonnieres.

Chris and her husband, Steve, also graciously invited me to move in with them, rent free, the final month before my wedding so I could save money for the big day.

My sweet, wonderful seamstress friend Susan, who had been my roommate years before when I'd been engaged to someone else—who broke up with me a week before the wedding (read *Through the Rocky Road and into the Rainbow Sherbet* if you want details)—made my beautiful wedding veil. She traipsed to several florists in town, looking for just the right size and shade of baby pink roses to adorn my pretty handmade headpiece. Today, I have that gorgeous veil hanging in my office.

Katie, another of my bridesmaids, created our embossed wedding invitation for us, complete with her gorgeous calligraphy.

And Michael's sister Debbie, cake maker extraordinaire, made us the most glorious wedding cake I'd ever seen, based on a picture I'd cut out of *Victoria* magazine.

However, the morning of the wedding, Debbie decided she didn't like the look of the pale pink and blue frosting roses she'd been painstakingly crafting for weeks and weeks. Instead, she and her sister Sheri and the twins raced all over town to different florists, buying up all the fresh pink and white roses and beautiful white and blue-tinted daisies they could find to decorate the cake. The result was exquisite, with a cascade of fresh flowers tumbling down one whole side of the cake. It looked even more gorgeous than the magazine picture.

Thank you, Debbie, for that stunning, unforgettable gift.

My mom and my sister, Lisa, joined together to give me several wonderful gifts and mementos for the wedding day: a pretty floral guest book, a quill-feathered pen to sign the guest book with, and a lovely wedding album to document every bridal moment. Also, knowing how much I love antique or old-fashioned things (my gown was Victorian-style ivory satin and lace), they gave me a pair of beautiful pearl and marcasite earrings, a gorgeous Victorian pearl and marcasite brooch, and ivory satin fingerless "gloves" that looped around my thumbs. (I think there's a particular name for those fingerless gloves, but for the life of me, I don't know what it is. If you do, please end my suspense and write and tell me at Ljenwalk@aol.com. Thanks!)

Lana, my maid of honor, did countless things to help in the months and days leading up to the wedding. But what I'm most grateful for was spending my last single night at her apartment, where we got to have some important best girlfriend time.

With Lana's wedding—where I was the matron of honor—there was a last-minute crisis the night before. After the rehearsal dinner, several of us had gone over to the church to decorate the reception room, and Lana was expecting her soon-to-be-groom, Michael (yes, she married a Michael, too), at any minute, but he was late arriving.

When his best man arrived, Lana asked him where her almost-groom was.

"He was tired and said he was going home to bed," he replied.

Lana lost it.

Upset, she asked the best man to please tell Michael that he needed to get over to the church. Soon.

When a confused and tired Michael—who'd coached his daughter's softball tournament that day—arrived, the couple exchanged words. Michael said, "But you already had lots of people helping . . . ," and a teary Lana told her groom that since it was *their* wedding, she'd expected that they'd romantically work together side-by-side preparing for the big day.

"Michael couldn't understand what the big deal was," Lana remembered, "and I thought, *Okay, is this how it's going to be our entire married life?*" Eventually, they kissed and made up, with Michael staying to help.

That night when she went to bed, Lana slept with her clothes on. She was thinking of making a quick getaway the next morning.

When she woke up, however, she found a note from Michael

124

shoved beneath her door that said, "Please forgive me. I love you, and I really want to marry you."

A still upset but in love Lana showed me the note when I came to pick her up a little while later, not understanding how Michael could have been so thoughtless and insensitive the night *before* the wedding.

I took my best friend out for breakfast, and with all the wisdom of an old married woman—of two years—and a wealth of experience in the *Dated Jekyll, Married Hyde* area, I gently explained that Michael hadn't deliberately set out to be thoughtless or insensitive; he was simply being a guy.

In other words, clueless.

> *That night when she went to bed, Lana slept with her clothes on. She was thinking of making a quick getaway the next morning.*

"It's just one of those male-female things," I told Lana, adding that it had probably never even entered Michael's mind that she'd want him there, because decorating's a girl thing. Plus, he was tired and had a big day coming up—one of the most important days of his life. And a big night as well. He wanted to be well rested.

This story has a happy ending. My friends married that day in a lovely ceremony and have now been happily living together as husband and wife for nearly a decade—with Michael a helpful co-laborer in the marriage, sharing household responsibilities and tasks.

Although Lana takes charge of the decorating.

The weekend before my friend Jan's wedding, her maid of honor and best friend, Jeanne, kidnapped her and took her to a cabin up at Lake Tahoe, their last outing together as single "sisters."

"As we sat in front of a roaring fire, all these jumbled emotions came gushing out," Jan recalled. "We felt like Siamese twins, facing the loss of our second selves, uncertain how our friendship would have to change. There would be no more 5:00 A.M. phone calls, no more popping over in pajamas for movie night, or her leaving me a message saying, 'It's payback time. Set up the Scrabble board.' My focus would be on building a marriage; Jeanne would form a new circle of friends and activities.

"This chapter of our lives was coming to a close, and we had to grieve," Jan said. "That's why on my wedding eve, after writing my vows, I penned a letter to Jeanne. I cried as I recounted all our antics together, the way she buoyed me with her cheerfulness and how she will always have a special place in my heart that no one else can fill—not even my husband."

Our husbands, whom we become one with in the sanctified bonds of marriage, are our cherished partners, lovers, and friends. But if not for the love, help, and time of our wedding

126

wonder-women girlfriends, most of us would never make it through the wedding day.

> Each one should use whatever gift he has received
> to serve others, faithfully administering God's grace
> in its various forms.

Girl Pearls Single but wanting to see what you'd look like in a wedding dress? Grab your best friend and go try on wedding gowns in the bridal department of your favorite store. (Or rent *Muriel's Wedding* or *My Big Fat Greek Wedding* to see the wedding dresses you wouldn't be caught dead in.) Already married? Take a stroll down wedding memory lane and look at each other's wedding pictures or videos. If you've never arranged your photos from that big day, schedule a fun scrapbooking or Creative Memories session one afternoon with another procrastinating girlfriend while you relive happy moments and get organized at the same time.

10

The Diaper Change

How a little bundle of joy can change
a friendship.

To have a friend is to have one of the sweetest gifts
that life can bring: to be a friend is to have a solemn
and tender education of soul from day to day.

Chinese Proverb

know I take my life into my hands as I say this, but . . . I'm not a baby person. Never have been.

Ever.

But before you ask me to turn in my fine-example-of-Christian-womanhood lifetime membership card, know this: I can't help it.

When God was dispensing those maternal instinct genes—particularly toward newborns—he bypassed me. Proof positive: When I was little and all the girls my age were playing with baby dolls and doll buggies, I was across the street busily vroom-vrooming Tonka trucks with Jeff Willis, the neighbor boy.

When I was growing up, whenever a new baby joined our extended family ranks, all the other female family members would coo, smile, talk baby talk to the beloved infant, and reach out eager arms to hold the precious little bundle of joy. I'd smile politely at the usually crying babe, murmur a few words of appreciation—"Cute . . . sweet . . ."—then quickly return to my Trixie Belden or Nancy Drew. I never understood the fascination.

Or the desire everyone had to hold it—um, her or him.

"Can I hold her please?"

"My turn now."

"Come to Grandma, sweet pea." Blah, blah, blah.

Eventually, the new mother would approach me, glowing with love and pride, eagerly extend her wrinkled little darling to me, and say, "Laura, would you like to hold your new little cousin/second cousin/third cousin twice removed?"

Knowing I was being granted a great honor and, unwilling to offend—especially under the watchful female family eyes that had all swiveled my direction—I'd smile and mumble, "Uh, sure."

"You have to put your book down first, Laura."

But I'll lose my place.

"Make sure you support his head, now."

Oh, no—what if I drop him?!

"Just think. Someday, you'll have your own sweet little baby like this!"

Doubt it. At least not 'til I'm really, really old—thirty maybe.

"Look—see how he has his daddy's chin?"

He does?

"But he's got his mother's nose," interrupts the proud grandma.

"You're right," they'd all agree.

I'd look politely at the fidgety babe in my arms, but all I could see was a squashy little scrunched-up red face that bore no resemblance to anyone I knew.

Thirty-some years later, all babies still look alike to me.

Sure, some are longer and thinner, others are shorter and plumper, some have a wonderful shock of thick, dark hair, and others are basically bald or maybe have pale-blond peach fuzz, but aside from that, they all look pretty much the same to me.

"Seven-and-a-half pounds and nineteen inches!" the new mom, dad, or grandparent will proudly call to announce.

I never know what that means.

And when it's up to me to pass on this important information to friends or family members, I always get it wrong—unless I remember to write it down. The problem is twofold for me, babies AND numbers. Two things I know little about.

"Just remember, honey," Michael will explain, "that's a little longer than a football."

But don't get me wrong here. It's not that I DISLIKE babies, not at all. In fact, I'm thrilled and delighted for friends and family when they have their blessed event, knowing how much it means to them—especially if they've been trying for a long time to get pregnant. (Heartfelt congratulations on your twins, Rebecca!) And I share in their joy and rejoice with them.

I just don't *know* much about babies.

Case in point: A few years ago I was at a writers' conference, sitting around a table, talking to a male editor and a group of women writers, including one young, very pregnant woman.

In the course of our conversation, Rene, the mother-to-be, mentioned the words "Braxton Hicks."

"Oh," I said politely, "is that what you're planning to name your baby?"

The whole table—including my male editor, father of three daughters—cracked up.

"Braxton Hicks is the name of a false contraction," Rene explained.

What can I say? I'm a stranger in a strange land—babyland.

I've simply never been around babies much—nor do I have any of my own, and most of my friends who are my age (mid-forties) either don't have children or their kids are already grown, or near-grown.

Like my best friend Lana, who became an instant stepmom to two teens when she married her husband, Michael, nearly a decade ago. The kids have since become adults and moved out on their own.

I'm a stranger in a strange land— babyland.

And my friend Katie.

Katie and I have been friends for ages. We met more than fifteen years ago when we were in singles leadership together at church. She's kind, generous, and bubbly and is a gifted poet with her own greeting card line.

Our friendship has flourished over time.

When I quit my secretarial job in my early thirties to rejoin the ranks of starving college students in a last-ditch attempt to get my degree, she'd feed me delicious manicotti dinners and give me a deep discount on her greeting cards—as in free—whenever a friend or family member's birthday was coming up.

She was a bridesmaid in my wedding, and a few years later when I got the contract for my first book, *Dated Jekyll, Married Hyde,* she graciously made the offer to be my "first reader."

I took her up on it in a New York minute, because not only is Katie a fellow writer, she's also fall-down-on-the-floor funny. (Since I was writing a humor book, having a funny person's input was critical.)

Plus, she lives in the gorgeous Sonoma Valley of California. AND she always feeds me well when I come to visit—wonderful homemade soups and pastas, yummy breads and bagels, and lots and lots of to-die-for chocolate chip cookies.

It became a ritual. I'd begin work on a new book and go visit Katie at her wonderful home with a view in Sebastopol. She'd brainstorm chapter ideas and titles with me and whip up delicious homemade meals while I wrote all morning long and into the early afternoon.

Then we'd break for lunch, and I'd give her my pages to review.

Her common refrain was always, "Make this funnier" or "Tighten this up!"

I loved making the two-and-a-half-hour drive from Sacramento through California's gorgeous wine country for my fun and productive writing getaways at Katie's.

And then poof—everything changed overnight.

And I mean overnight.

Suddenly, and with no warning, over a twelve-hour time period my forty-something friend Katie became mom to a newborn baby.

One of her close family members had gotten pregnant and had come to the difficult decision to put the baby up for adoption. When the baby was due to be born, Katie went to show her support and to meet this precious new addition who would only be with the family a brief twenty-four hours before going to her new home.

As she made the four-hour drive to be there for the birth, Katie's emotions ran high. She was excited and at the same time she grieved at the family's losing this child so quickly. Additionally, and unexpectedly, feelings of disappointment for her own loss of never having been blessed with a baby overcame her.

But Katie snapped out of it, quickly putting aside her feelings so as to be supportive for the rest of the family at this bittersweet time.

Little did she know then that God was about to bless her

in a way that she would never even allow herself to dream of. Miraculously, at the eleventh hour, God intervened in the adoption process. Now instead of leaving Katie's family, little Jacqueline would *become* her family—*her* daughter, the very next day.

Now, I'd known Katie was going down to see the baby, and in fact, she'd even e-mailed me, "It's a girl!" So a couple days later when she called and excitedly squealed, "I have a baby!" I replied, "I know. You already told me. Congratulations on the new addition to the family."

"No. *I* have a baby!"

"WHAT?!"

Then she told me the whole amazing story I've just told you. Can you say, "BIG surprise"? I was speechless.

Both Katie and I were in our mid-forties and knew we'd never have children—which was fine. God's plan and all that. And we were content. Besides, Katie had already step-parented Mark's two daughters, Ingrid and Julia, and loved every minute—well, nearly every minute—of being a second mom through the girls' teenage years. She adores the girls, and the feeling is mutual.

But she'd never raised a child from infancy. Now here she was instant mom to a newborn, baby Jacqueline.

That was the day our friendship changed.

After I got over the initial shock—which happened just minutes into that phone call—we both shed happy tears. I

136

shared in her excitement by immediately going out and buying pretty, girly baby gifts for little Jacqueline.

But then after that initial important phone call, I didn't hear from Katie.

For ages.

My sweet, funny writing friend who used to call me several times a month "just to chat" or to discuss mutual writing projects now maintained a strict phone silence—never calling, never returning any of my messages.

And as for e-mail? Forget it. It was like she'd dropped off the face of the earth. Katie was completely incommunicado for the first six or seven weeks of little Jacqueline's life.

And I didn't get it.

Having never had a baby, I couldn't understand how it could consume her *every* waking minute. (Okay, all you moms, stop laughing right now!)

What I didn't know then was that Katie—who, like me, had never been around newborns much—was going through a crash course of on-the-job training in learning how to take care of a baby, which left no room for the normal, everyday things of life like phone calls and e-mail and friendship.

Had I ever been a mom, I'd have understood. But I hadn't, and I couldn't. (Although I wisely didn't share that with Katie, figuring she had enough on her plate to deal with already.)

A couple months after little Jacqueline became a member

of the family, I drove to Sebastopol for Katie's after-the-fact baby shower. I intended to stay a few days as I always did—and I brought my newest manuscript to work on and to get her feedback as I always did also.

But the "always" was no longer. Everything had changed.

I was delighted to meet pretty little Jacqueline—Jackie—and even more delighted to see the joy she'd brought to my friend's life. Katie was besotted with her new baby and the happiest I'd ever seen her—other than when she was falling in love with and marrying Mark.

She radiated motherly love and joy, which was a wonderful blessing to see.

But after about seven or eight hours of nonstop baby focus—looking at the baby, playing with the baby, talking to the baby, talking ABOUT the baby—the blessing began to wear a little thin.

When Katie put Jackie down for her nap, I was pleased that we'd finally have some time for a little girl talk.

And we did.

Only the girl talk was mostly about her little girl. My friend was over the moon about her new daughter.

And I tried to relate, really I did.

But it wasn't the same as when Katie fell in love with Mark and gave me detailed minute-by-minute descriptions of their courtship—and I did the same with mine and Michael's. That was something we'd *both* experienced and were appropriately romantically gooey and giddy over.

But all this baby stuff was uncharted, foreign territory to me, the woman who as a child had preferred Tonka trucks over baby dolls.

So after leaving that weekend—after staying only a day and a half and not working on my manuscript at all—I wept on the drive home over what I perceived had to be the loss of our friendship. Katie wasn't the least bit interested in writing anymore—and that had always been one of our strongest connections. As a new mom, her focus was 100 percent on her baby—which is as it should be—but to a non-mom, non–baby person who wasn't living, sleeping, breathing babyhood, I couldn't imagine what we had in common anymore.

And it made me sad.

After that trip, I knew things would never be the same again. But I also knew that I couldn't talk to Katie about it. She was on a new-mother high, and it would have been selfish of me to say anything to dilute that joy. This was a special bonding time between her, Mark, and their new baby, and I didn't want to say or do anything to spoil that. So I kept quiet and resigned myself to the fact that things change, people change, and therefore, friendships change—even when we don't want them to.

The reality was that as much as I loved my friend Katie, I simply couldn't relate to the baby thing.

Toddlers are a different story altogether. There's something about them that simply melts my heart.

Show me a toddler who waddles around in that cute-little-dimpled-thigh toddler walk or giggles and says a few adorably mispronounced words here and there, and I'm smitten.

Take J. P., the little boy next door with his curly, dark brown hair, big brown eyes, and long, dark lashes.

I adore him.

He's our little Dennis the Menace—only so much cuter—always coming over for cookies or bananas and to visit our dog, Gracie. "Gacie, Gacie," he used to say appealingly whenever he saw her (before he could say his *r*'s.)

How cute is that?

J. P. and I have a ritual whenever we say good-bye—we blow kisses to each other.

One day when he blew me an especially big kiss, I grabbed my cheek dramatically and staggered back a few steps, saying, "Wow! That was a really big kiss. It almost knocked me over."

Now when he blows me kisses, he always says, "You have to fall over!"

J. P. reminds me a lot of my nephew Josh with his dark hair and big, dark eyes. When Josh was three and I'd spend the night on their couch, he'd cuddle up to me and say, "I wuv you, Aunt Waura."

I miss those days. He's twenty-six now and hasn't said "wuv you" in years.

My sister-in-law Sheri, a well-read, intelligent woman, has always been a practical, straightforward, no-nonsense—some would say blunt—kind of gal, not given easily to sentiment.

Then her first grandchild, Alexandria (Lexi), was born.

And I saw an ooooey-gooey sentimental side of Sheri I'd never seen before. Suddenly, she was snapping pictures every second. "Lexi, look at Grandma . . ." "Oh look at her asleep on Daddy's chest—I need a picture of that," "Isn't she adorable in her new outfit?" etc., etc.

What a change.

Even Michael, who's always been like a second dad to his twin nieces, Kari and Jennie—and with Lexi's birth is now a surrogate "grandpa"—got into the act.

"Can I hold her?" he eagerly asked new mom Jennie the first time we met little Lexi in the hospital.

Everyone was absolutely gaga over the baby.

Except me, of course.

I mean, she was cute and everything, and I was thrilled and happy for her parents, grandparents, and my husband, who took such a delight in his new great-niece and, like his sister, started pulling out the camera *every* time he saw the baby.

But even though Lexi was related to me—the daughter of my niece, whom I dearly love—she was still a baby.

And like I said, I just don't "get" babies.

Then I went over to visit one night when she was about four months old . . . and Lexi smiled right up at me. That did it. I was a goner. I played with her much of the night.

But that still didn't mean I *knew* any more about babies. At one point in the evening, her Aunt Kari—my then twenty-three-year-old niece—had been feeding Lexi, and she'd fallen asleep. Imagine my surprise when she awoke a short while later.

"Why is it that when she's asleep, then she wakes up?" I asked Kari and Jennie cluelessly.

And my twin nieces burst out laughing.

"Aunt Laura, why is it that when *you're* asleep, then you wake up?" said Kari with a straight face as Jennie giggled.

"But I thought after you fed a baby and she fell asleep, she was down for the whole night."

I had a lot to learn about babies.

The good news is that recently I went to see Katie and Jackie, a few weeks after Jackie's first birthday, and this time, I fell head over heels.

From the moment I got out of the car and Katie came to meet me with her golden-haired child in her arms, I was in love. Jackie tilted her sweet little head to one side and giggled—just like her mom. She's got to be the smilingest child I've ever seen. (At least I thought so until Lexi grinned up at me.)

142

As I lay on the floor, playing and giggling with little Jackie, Katie raised her eyebrows and teased, "Is this my same friend who was here last time and not too interested in my baby?"

"But she's not a *baby* anymore," I said. "She's a toddler. And her own little person. She walks and talks, giggles and laughs, and gives sweet little kisses now."

That day when Katie put Jackie down for a nap, we had a nice long chat over a cup of tea and both gently explained what it was like for each of us.

Katie told me how terrifying it was in the beginning to be responsible for this little baby who couldn't do anything for herself. My friend did not have nine months to prepare like most moms do. She didn't even have one week. She had a scant twelve hours to adjust to the reality of becoming a mom.

And suddenly she had to learn *every*thing overnight. It was a scary and overwhelming responsibility.

Then I told her how my entire life I've never been drawn to babies—it had nothing to do with *her* baby. But now that I'd spent time with Jackie as a toddler, it was a different story.

I'm happy to say that my friendship with Katie is now back on an even keel and we were able to pick up right where we left off. We're as close as we used to be, and I'm crazy about her little Jackie. And the three of us enjoy some great girl time together.

Although I still don't volunteer to change diapers.

> It is very easy to forgive others their mistakes; it takes more grit and gumption to forgive them for having witnessed your own.
>
> *Jessamyn West*

Girl Pearls Don't allow a major change in your girlfriend's life to end your friendship. Find a creative way to adapt, or incorporate this important life change into your usual girl time. For instance, if, like me, you're childless—or your children are already grown—and a dear, longtime friend suddenly becomes a mom, when you go to visit, spend time playing with the baby and hold off on your girlfriend talk until the baby goes down for a nap. Or, if you need a little longer one-on-one chat time with your friend, pay her favorite baby-sitter, then spirit your new-mom-friend away to a café for an hour or two for some chocolate and conversation.

11

My Mother, My Friend

Although our mothers may make us crazy
sometimes, it's great when we grow up
and can become friends with them.

Holy as heaven a mother's tender love, the love of many prayers
and many tears which changes not with dim, declining years.

Caroline Norton

Remember how when you were a little girl you adored your mom, played with her makeup, and wanted to be just like her? And then came those teenage days when your mom made you crazy and you fought with her over makeup, boys, and curfew. But the best days of all are now, when you're all grown up and she's not just your mother but also your friend.

My mom and I are better friends today than ever. We either talk or e-mail nearly every day and get together for lunch—except when I'm on deadline—a few times a month.

We've also been on a few trips together—to Arizona, San Diego, and other parts of southern California. But the one neither of us will ever forget is when Mom accompanied Michael and me on my first book tour and we got to "do" New York City together.

It was incredible—going to the top of the Empire State Building, visiting the Metropolitan Museum of Art, walking through Central Park, eating the best cheesecake in the world at the Carnegie Deli, enjoying a lovely afternoon tea at the St. Regis (the Plaza was booked), and best of all, seeing *Les Miserables* on Broadway.

We had an amazing, unforgettable time—which I'll talk more about later.

146

And then, before we hit the Chicago leg of the tour, we had the opportunity to spend the weekend in our old hometown of Racine, Wisconsin, and Mom was able to see relatives she hadn't seen in nearly thirty years. It was a happy reunion, especially when she got to visit her beloved older sister Lucille.

We have wonderful memories, and lots of photos, to remind us of that special time. Mom and I loved reconnecting with both sides of the family and seeing the houses of our respective youths. We drove by the wooden two-story house where she grew up with her siblings, and she pointed out her old bedroom window to me, as well as the driveway where she and my dad—who died when I was fifteen—used to neck.

Happy mom times.

Cathleen Snyder, a former colleague of mine, says there's no one in the world she's closer to than her mom. "We have always been friends as well as mother and daughter," Cathleen said. "My mom was strict when I needed it, but for the most part, she treated me as someone she respected and genuinely liked, which allowed us to develop an excellent relationship."

That relationship became even stronger when Cathleen's mom was diagnosed with breast cancer and her dad died unexpectedly four years later.

"The first year after my dad died was very difficult for

Mom. Although she has always been quite independent, she really didn't know where to turn, and I didn't know what to do to help her," Cathleen recalled. "It suddenly struck me one day that she and my dad had never really traveled and that she might like to see some places she had never seen. She agreed, somewhat reluctantly, to go on a road trip with me that spring. So early one May morning, we loaded the dog into the car and took off.

"I took her to some places I had been that I knew she would like—Yellowstone National Park, Grand Teton National Park, and the Wasatch Mountains of Utah—and some places I had always wanted to go—Santa Fe, New Mexico, and southern Colorado. From the horrible motel in the dead-end town of Nowheresville, Utah, to the treacherous drive down the steep, wet back roads into Jackson Hole, Wyoming, we had a ball every minute of the way.

"After that, our trips became a yearly ritual," Cathleen said. "One year we drove the Pacific Northwest—from Oregon to Washington to British Columbia, and even to Victoria on Vancouver Island.

"My mom now cares for her eighty-seven-year-old mother, so there will be no more vacations for a while. Nevertheless, I cherish all the memories from those trips we've taken. And someday, we'll take the rest of the trips we've planned—with or without fleabag motels!"

148

My niece Kari also enjoys traveling with her mother—my sister-in-law Sheri.

"My mom's my movie friend and traveling buddy," Kari said. "The first trip we went on together was to Chicago when I was eighteen. My mom had a business trip, and I tagged along. That's when I'd just started liking museums and art and 'girly things,' as Mom called it. We stayed at the Drake Hotel and got to go to the Chicago Art Institute, where I saw Monet's *Water Lilies* and Seurat's *Sunday in the Park with George*."

Kari and her mom also went on their first trip to Europe together. Sheri had wanted to visit Europe her entire life—particularly in her twenties—but circumstances and finances had never permitted. Now at the age of fifty-two, she finally got to go—to England. The experience was all the sweeter because she got to share it with her twenty-four-year-old daughter.

A few months before their trip, Sheri decided to buy Kari good luggage as a Christmas present. "She knew that once I went to England, I'd want to go back," Kari said, "so she got me a four-piece set of American Tourister luggage. Then she went back and got herself some, since she'd be traveling, too."

Sheri also bought Kari a care package of trip-related "stocking stuffers"—a rain slicker, clothesline, ear plugs, Tylenol, hand sanitizer, a small photo album so Kari could carry pictures of her new niece Lexi, gum, and toilet seat covers.

The latter made her very popular with the rest of the tour members.

Kari's twin, Jennie, said she was about fifteen when she first realized her mom was her friend. "She was crying about something, and I really wanted to cheer her up," Jennie recalled. "Not because she was my mom, but because I cared about her as a person. And it dawned on me then that I considered her my friend. And I was like, 'Whoa!' but it made me really happy.

"My mom and I have always been close," Jennie said, "but I remember, one day when I was about four years old, she said something I didn't like. I was in the back seat of the car, and I looked at her in the rearview mirror and said, 'I hate you, Mom!' And my mom said, 'Well, I love you!' I was holding my prayer bear at the time, and I looked at it and felt so bad and guilty for being mean to my mommy. I looked up at her with tears in my eyes and said, 'I don't hate you, Mommy. I love you.' I learned then never to say those words in anger again."

Although my Texas friend Annette and her mom also had their struggles when she was growing up, they now enjoy a close, loving relationship. "She's my biggest cheerleader and fan and is always encouraging me," Annette said.

She recalled the time when her mom accompanied her to

150

a speaking event in Minnesota. "Once I'd done my speaking thing, we went shopping," Annette said. "There were lots of cute, arty, expensive little shops, and in one I spotted a tiny silver pin that I just longed for. It was a small star, and suspended from it was a postage-stamp-sized piece of silver hand stamped with the words *Carpe Diem* ("seize the day") on it. I love unusual, symbolic jewelry, and I love words—especially those words; I try to live by them—but the pin was a handmade original and expensive," Annette said. "Too much for me to spend, so I passed it up.

"When we returned home to Texas, my mom spent the night at my house before driving home. After she left, I went in to change her bedding, and I found a small gift-wrapped box with the pin inside.

"Now every time I wear the pin, I think of her."

Her proud mom, who is an artist, also helped her storytelling daughter out by painting "Once upon a time . . ." above the windows in Annette's office.

It's great to have a cheerleading mom who delights in your accomplishments.

My mom keeps a framed poster from my first book signing in her home office. It's great to have a cheerleading mom who delights in your accomplishments.

The evening that Mom, Michael, and I arrived in New York on my book tour, our taxi drove by Lincoln Center, the home of the Metropolitan Opera, where we noticed that the incredible Placido Domingo was currently appearing. Opera lover Michael was thrilled to see the Center for the first time, yet at the same time, terribly disappointed because he knew that his favorite tenor was performing in that building at that very moment.

"So close and yet so far," Michael said wistfully, hand touching the window of the cab.

Placido Domingo is Mom's favorite classical singer, too, so we briefly discussed the prospect of getting to see the great tenor while we were in town, but I had a full publicity schedule with no free evenings. However, there was one evening when I had a speaking engagement that Mom and Michael might be able to go to the opera without me.

"But don't you want us to come hear you speak?" Mom asked.

"You've heard me speak a zillion times. How often do you get the chance to see Placido Domingo? At the Metropolitan Opera, no less?"

"Okay, well we'll see how expensive the tickets are and then decide," Mom said.

The tickets were exorbitant—well beyond our combined budgets, so that was that.

Or so Mom thought.

When Michael and I discussed it privately, at first we agreed that it was an extravagance we couldn't afford. But then I thought, *Who knows when, or if, we'll ever get back to New York again? And who knows when we'll get the chance to see Placido Domingo again?* So I told Michael, "This calls for drastic steps—pull out the plastic." (We'd agreed not to charge things on our credit card unless it was an emergency.)

But this qualified. It was a once-in-a-lifetime, memory-making entertainment emergency. "Charge 'em, honey," I said.

So the arrangements were made—without Mom's knowledge—through our publicist's ticket broker.

Late in the afternoon on the day of the performance, Mom wanted to discuss dinner plans before we had to leave for my speaking engagement. But Michael said slyly, "Mom, how would you like to go out on a date with your son-in-law instead?"

"But aren't we going to hear Laura speak?"

Then he told her our surprise while I watched to see her reaction.

Mom couldn't believe it. "You can't afford that!" she said.

"I asked you out on a date," Michael said. "It's not polite to talk about the cost."

Dinner was promptly forgotten—they grabbed a hot dog on the run—and not until they got to the theater did they see their tickets and discover they were sitting in the FRONT

ROW. CENTER. AT THE MET! They could almost touch the conductor.

The two people I love most in the world got to see their favorite singer in the world on the stage of one of the most renowned opera houses in the world.

It doesn't get much better than that.

> May your father and mother be glad;
> may she who gave you birth rejoice!
>
> *Proverbs 23:25*

Girl Pearls Arrange a fun girlfriend time with your mom. Dress up and take her to the ballet, a play, or other cultural event, and then discuss it afterward over coffee or tea and some decadently delicious dessert. If your mom is no longer living or doesn't live nearby, adopt a mom (someone from your neighborhood, church, or nursing home) and take her out instead.

12

Working Girls

Our nine-to-five friendships enrich our lives
and help us make it through the workday.

Work is something you can count on,
a trusted lifelong friend who never deserts you.

Margaret Bourke-White

hen what happened?"

"He changed his mind again! And now I have to start from scratch once more. Can you believe it?"

"Yep. Been there. Done that. Tell you what . . . let's order dessert today. We need it after the awful week we've had."

Commiserating about a difficult boss over lunch with a woman friend from work can be a lifesaver.

Not to mention a good way to stay employed.

Work girlfriends hold a special friendship spot in our lives. They can be encouraging mentors, sympathetic ears, and fun comrades-in-arms. Sometimes, they're simply friends for a season while we work together, and we don't socialize out of the work place. Other times, we get together for the occasional lunch, dinner, wedding, or baby shower. And still other times, we become lifelong friends.

My friend Lisa is one of the latter.

We met when we job-shared a part-time secretarial position at church more than a decade ago. Lisa is blond, beautiful, and bubbly. And she's one of the most positive people I've ever known. That woman always has a smile on her face. If you looked up *encourager* in the dictionary, you'd find Lisa's picture.

When we worked together, I was finishing up my journalism degree at the university and would often confide in Lisa about my dreams of someday becoming an author—a dream that seemed fantastical and way beyond my secretarial reach.

"You'll do it. I know you will," Lisa would say with her sparkling smile. "I can already see it. And then I can tell everybody I knew you when."

Lisa also shared with me her dreams of someday owning her own business where she could put her excellent organizational talents to use.

Nearly fifteen years later, both of our dreams have come true. I'm a full-time author and speaker, and Lisa is now the proud owner of a time and organizational management company. We stay in touch by phone or the occasional lunch, and recently I hired her to help organize my messy home office.

She's amazing. And I'm honored to call her my friend.

Jamie and I also met at work.

When I began a new job at a publishing company in my early forties, most of the people I worked with were fresh out of college and spoke a totally different language than I did—particularly when it came to music, movies, and social habits.

I felt isolated, out of it—and old—in my little cubicle.

But then I met Jamie—another beautiful blond—who was a few years older than me and also a writer, and we became fast friends. Even though she was a single mom with grown kids and I was married with no kids, we had shared interests and tastes. (She knew who Doris Day, Andy Williams, and the singing King Family were. In fact, I was surprised and delighted to learn that Jamie was a MEMBER of the King Family. Her mom, Donna, was one of the original four King sisters, and Jamie herself sang in countless King Family specials in the '60s—which I used to always watch on TV.) Wow! I couldn't believe it. One of the King Family girls was now my friend! How cool is that?

Jamie and I would often go to lunch or take breaks together when work permitted. And even though I quit that job a few years ago to become a full-time writer, we still get together for lunch when we can and have fun catching up. (And Jamie, one of these days I'm going to get you to show me some of those old black-and-white King Family shows.)

Susan and I were also work pals. A few years ago when I was working at a thankless, not-very-well-paying job for a demanding, unappreciative boss, my coworker Susan—who was also overworked and underappreciated—and I became walking buddies.

Sometimes it was just to exercise and get some fresh air, but more often it was to get away from the office and go where we could vent and walk off our frustrations. We'd take turns encouraging each other and reminding ourselves that we were intelligent, talented women with a lot to offer.

Happily, others saw that, too, and we both left for more fulfilling—and better paying—jobs for which we were more suited.

When my best friend Lana, a teacher and a jock, first began teaching at her school (when she was still single), she became friends with Maria, the school counselor—now a principal—who was also single. And athletic.

Unlike me.

Lana—who for some reason felt the physical need to keep up her sporty status and athleticism—and Maria liked to get together on the weekends to do such fun outdoor activities as run, bicycle, and ski.

The two working-girl friends ran the Bay to Breakers ten-kilometer race one year—where thousands of runners run from one end of San Francisco through the city to the other end, up and down those steep hills in the City by the Bay. "That was an experience," Lana recalled. "You're running along, and you run past a group of naked people, or others in all kinds of costumes—like Trekkies in their Star Trek uniforms."

Lana and Maria also participated in a memorable hundred-kilometer bike ride in Napa Valley that started at 7 A.M. Apparently, there are different kinds of bikes that do different kinds of things: mountain bikes for short hilly or mountainous rides, and road bikes—like the one Lance Armstrong, the multi-winning Tour de France champion, rides—for long, grueling races. "The people on the road bikes were finished by eleven o'clock," Lana said, "but we were on mountain bikes, so we didn't get finished until two in the afternoon. At the twenty-five-mile marker, you could have gotten in a van and gone back, but we thought, *We can make it.*

"But at about thirty miles, we knew we'd made a huge mistake," Lana recalled. "We wound up riding and walking the rest of the way. We were in excruciating pain, going up and down hills. Plus, we had on tank tops and hadn't put on any sunscreen, so we had major sunburns on our shoulders.

"When we got finished, the first thing we did was take Tylenol."

And Lana wonders why I'm not into sports.

Lana, who teaches special ed at a small school out in the country, and her teaching assistant Ana have been working-girl friends for nearly fifteen years.

Although they started out in different places in their lives—Lana was single and in her early thirties; Ana was married with two kids and in her late twenties—their lives have become pretty parallel over the years.

"When I got married and became a stepmom, we had teenagers at the same time and we went through those same teenage difficulties at the same time," Lana said. "Also, our

160

mothers-in-law both have a lot of health problems, and our spouses are the children who've taken on the primary responsibility for making sure those parents are taken care of."

Lana and Ana have forged a deep bond over the years—formed in part by the singular demands, challenges, and joys of working with special needs children—and although they rarely get together outside of school, they both appreciate and rely on their special working-girl friendship.

Many years ago my friend Lonnie left the teaching profession and took a job at a book distributor in Michigan. She started working in a department of thirty women and two men and then moved to a department of eight women headed by a man who kept a "Do Not Disturb" sign on his door.

This was the first time I'd ever worked with so many women, and it was an experience I'll never forget. I learned to refrigerate pantyhose before wearing them (it extends the life).

"We were pretty much on our own," Lonnie recalled. "This was the first time I'd ever worked with so many women, and it was an experience I'll never forget. I learned to refrigerate pantyhose before wearing them (it extends the life). And the potlucks were phenomenal. None of us was paid much, so whenever someone had a baby, the showers the coworkers threw—always during work hours—were huge affairs and very generous."

But there's one thing Lonnie remembers most from that time.

She was working her way up in a new career in publishing and had her sights set on New York City. After three years at the book distributor, she was offered an interview in Manhattan.

"I told the women in my department, and they were thrilled for me," Lonnie said. The day of the interview—"a stunning autumn day"—she walked the four blocks from her hotel in Manhattan to the company that was hiring. "I knew I wanted this job badly," Lonnie said, "if only to move to this amazing place." She arrived at the office building early and stood outside on the street, feeling sick to her stomach with nervousness.

Then she spied a phone booth.

Lonnie dialed her work's toll-free number and got connected to her department's secretary. "I told her I was standing on the street across from the publisher and I was scared to death to go inside," she said. "For the next ten minutes, every woman in that department took a turn on the phone to encourage me and boost me up."

Lonnie credits her calm during the interview to those women. She was hired that day on the spot.

Work girlfriends are a special blessing. They provide support and encouragement in the workplace, as well as a safe haven from the rigors of the job. And if we're very fortunate, they celebrate with us and cheer us on when we move on.

162

> To be successful, the first thing to do is fall in love
> with your work.

Sister Mary Lauretta

Girl Pearls Lunch is often the best time to get together with work girlfriends, so make it a treat. Try different restaurants, or for a fun surprise, pack a yummy picnic lunch and eat it in a nearby park. If there's no park or pretty outdoor area close by, have a car picnic in your work parking lot. The place isn't as important as taking the time to be with your friend to talk and take a break from the pressures of the work day. After lunch take a long walk—that way you get both exercise and conversation.

13

Pen Friends
and Long-Distance Relationships

The art of letter writing between friends
and how to keep those long-distance
relationships alive.

Writing creates a sanctuary. It is a place where friends,
although apart, can meet.

Sylvana Rosetti

Cathleen met her best friend Lisa in kindergarten. "We were the two shyest kids in the class," Cathleen recalls. "One day the class sat down in the circle, and no one sat next to me. A nasty little girl sneered and remarked that no one would want to sit by me. Tears burning in my eyes, I looked away and saw Lisa smiling shyly at me. I scooted over next to her, and a friendship was born."

Just before they entered the third grade, Lisa moved away to southern California. "I suspect most eight-year-olds would've drifted apart," Cathleen said, "but not Lisa and me. We were allowed to speak on the phone once a month—calls that consisted mostly of long silences, punctuated by comments like, 'My mom says I might get a Cabbage Patch Kid for Christmas if I'm good.'"

Cathleen visited Lisa twice during the four years she lived in southern California, and both times it was as if she had never moved away. When Lisa moved back to the Bay Area just before seventh grade, the friends picked up right where they left off and were best friends "as if we had never been apart."

Their friendship survived all the normal high school turmoil, and soon it was time to go off to college. Cathleen stayed at home and attended the local community college, but Lisa moved back to southern California to attend USC. The best friends spoke on the phone frequently but also wrote long letters detailing *every*thing. Those long missives somehow evolved into two individual, but inextricably linked, ongoing romantic dramas.

"At least once a week I wrote Lisa a new installment of the tumultuous love life of the fictional Charlotte and Alan," Cathleen said, "and each week Lisa wrote me an update of the Clint and Alex saga. Charlotte and Alex were best friends who had grown up together, so each character figured prominently in both stories. The tales were pure romantic cheese, but they were fun to write and even more fun to read.

"By the time Lisa moved back home a year later, the stories equaled *The Odyssey* in length, if not in literary prose," Cathleen said. "That Christmas, Lisa typed up my version of the story and had it spiral-bound into a little book, complete with a Harlequin-worthy cover. I found it not long ago and had a great laugh rereading it."

Lisa and Cathleen are still best friends, even though Lisa lives in Washington and Cathleen lives in California. The girlfriends e-mail almost every day, talk on the phone at least once a week, and visit whenever possible. "Maybe someday we'll have a horribly cheesy double wedding like the one in the Clint-Alex–Alan-Charlotte tales," Cathleen said with a laugh.

The only thing *I* can remember from kindergarten is taking wonderful naps on those red vinyl mats that we eagerly unfolded every afternoon—and my teacher's name, Mrs. Piggy-Toes. I mean Mrs. Piggins (but all us kids called her Mrs. Piggy-Toes to each other). I have no memories at all of any friends I made there, much less a best friend, although I know I must have had one. But we moved a lot when I was growing up, so a consistent friendship from kindergarten on was impossible.

I vaguely remember a best friend in the first grade—I think her name was Kathy Hansen—who loved to read as much as I did. We competed against one another to see who could read the most books *and* get the most gold stars on Miss Vopelensky's reading chart. I won—with 103 books—by the end of the first grade.

Joyce, a fifty-something friend of mine, also has a best friend from elementary school. "My friend Rose and I had always been in tune with each other," she said. "We've had this special friendship connection that's always been unbeatable. If I would be thinking about her, she would call me. If I picked up the phone and it was her, I would say, 'Well, did you get my message?' We have this special bond."

Recently Rose was in a very serious head-on collision.

"I received the message from one of her daughters that she was in critical condition and in a coma," Joyce recalled. "Her

168

husband also had been critically injured. Since I lived more than a hundred miles away, I couldn't see her."

Now, Joyce is a big believer in prayer, so when she took her daily walks, she would pray for Rose. "I sensed that she felt my prayers, and I knew that my prayers were being heard," Joyce said. "I longed to be with her, but because of my work and family, it was impossible. Then one day when I was writing in my journal, I thought that I could write a thirty-day journal to my girlfriend. When she got better, I could give it to her as a gift. It was therapeutic for me. I wrote a poem, told some jokes, or recalled humorous incidents about our growing up years together . . . Some pages were tearstained."

Joyce finally got to see Rose when she came home from the hospital. "What a joy-filled reunion," Joyce said. "I can't tell you how much the journal meant to my schoolmate buddy. I read some selected passages to her, and we laughed and cried together. The impact of sharing your life with someone, even if it is only for a short period of time, is a most treasured gift of love."

Although I might not remember my grade school friends, I still keep in touch with my sixth-grade teacher, Miss Vanderbrug—um, Jill. (She asked me to call her that when we reconnected in my early twenties, but I can't help myself. I still think of her as Miss Vanderbrug.)

I was twenty-three and fresh out of the Air Force when

I went back to my Wisconsin hometown for a visit. On a whim while staying at my aunt's house, I picked up the local phone book and looked under the *V*s to see if my favorite sixth-grade teacher was listed. Sure enough, there she was, at the same address where she'd lived when my family had moved away ten years earlier.

I called Miss Vanderbrug, and we got together and caught up with each others' lives. From then on, we began communicating across the miles through cards and letters. We still stay in touch today, only now it's mostly by e-mail.

Although I may not remember my grade school friends, I still keep in touch with my sixth grade teacher, Miss Vanderbrug—um, Jill.

My friend Karen, who admits she's not the greatest letter writer, says she thanks God every day for the Internet and e-mail. "Without it, I don't think I would stay in touch with as many of my girlfriends as I do."

Like her girlfriend Shannon, who was Karen's best friend in junior high and high school until she moved away to Maryland.

"We kept in contact for a couple years, but once I went away to college, we lost touch," Karen said. "That didn't mean I still didn't think of her often. I just didn't know how to get a hold of her—didn't know where she was."

170

Then, about a year ago, Karen was chatting with another friend from high school by e-mail who told her that Shannon had e-mailed her that very morning saying she'd randomly picked her name off the web site Classmates.com and was wondering if she knew Karen or how to get in touch with her.

"I couldn't believe that one of the very few people I keep in touch with from high school was the same one Shannon e-mailed!" Karen said. "My friend sent me Shannon's address, I immediately contacted her, and it was like we'd never stopped talking. Sure, we caught up on each other's lives, but girlfriends seem to have that 'thing' about them that enables them to go years without talking and then pick up as if it had only been a day. Now we write to each other on a weekly basis and have renewed a friendship that had been lost."

I have to credit the Internet, too—in particular, Classmates.com—for reconnecting me with my best friend from high school, Dawn Alexander, whom I hadn't had contact with in over twenty-five years.

A few months ago, I received an e-mail out of the blue from Dawn. Her husband—who's a couple years younger than her but had attended our high school—was scrolling through the Classmates web site and found my name, so he excitedly told Dawn, who'd been wanting to reach me for *years* but had no idea how. Now, thanks to the magic of technology, we have been reunited.

A lot had changed in the nearly thirty years since we'd last seen each other. We were both married, but Dawn had four kids—two of whom were in college—which was a little unbelievable to me, since as memories have a tendency to do, Dawn was still fixed in my mind's eye as my seventeen-year-old high school friend. What was she doing with FOUR KIDS?

We've since begun e-mailing back and forth and sharing photos—she's still as gorgeous and voluptuous as ever, the brat—and I'm hoping we can get together at our upcoming thirty-year high school reunion. But until then, cards and e-mail will suffice.

Leona, my twenty-something friend in Michigan, e-mails her sister Lue Ann, who lives in Florida, a lot.

"We make up some wacky stuff and just laugh ourselves silly," Leona said. "We had some e-mails going back and forth for a while called 'The Sister Show' where we shared strange tips and anecdotes with pretend 'listeners.' We pretended we were live on the air, talking to other women. The show was even complete with a sign-off statement: 'Thank you for joining us on the *Sister Show.* Have a mood-swing day filled with love and joy and tears . . . and blind rage and envy and spit."

But there are times when things aren't so wacky, like when

172

Lue Ann was struggling with depression. So her loving sister Leona put together a letter of Scripture and mailed it to her.

I used to be a huge letter writer.

I think it began when I was stationed overseas with the Air Force, long before the days of e-mail. The easiest, and cheapest, way to stay in touch—phone calls to and from the States were prohibitively expensive—was by writing letters.

Sunday afternoons, if I wasn't spending the weekend sightseeing, I'd gather together my favorite pen and a box of pretty stationery and stamps and spend several happy hours writing page after page of letters to friends and family. I had so much to tell—wonderful trips I'd taken (Paris, Amsterdam, Venice, Athens . . .), amazing sights I'd seen (the Swiss Alps, Holland's windmills, the Louvre . . .), and guys I was meeting. Oh, and of course, my work. Often, I'd write eleven- and twelve-page letters.

But it's been a long time since I've done that. Although I still love writing with beautiful stationery every now and then, these days I don't have the time to write lengthy letters. Instead, I'll send a nice card to special girlfriends to let them know I'm thinking about them. I like to personalize the envelope with whimsical or pretty stickers of flowers, teacups, or little sayings.

My seventy-something friend June is the consummate letter writer.

We met at the first writers' conference I attended nearly a decade ago and bonded over our mutual fear and trembling. Afterward, we began writing to one another—letters of encouragement, prayer requests, news of writing rejections or successes, what was going on in our families and our lives. We often shared favorite Scriptures or inspiring quotes, such as this one by Madeleine L'Engle: "God created me to write. I will write no matter what."

I always looked forward to June's letters, because there was no one else in my life who took the time to write by "snail mail" anymore. Most people preferred the phone. But as a woman in love with the written word, June's letters always meant a lot to me.

And to many others.

For over eighteen years, June wrote to missionaries in various countries. She was on the mission board at church and would send them monthly letters packed full of news of church activities and personal activities, what her family was doing, and her writing.

"After forty years, I still correspond with one of those missionaries and her various family members," June said. "She writes poetry, and usually each letter includes a poem. We still exchange personal family news and cares and concerns.

174

"For me, keeping in touch via words on paper links hearts and minds more personally than e-mail," June said.

"I like e-mail and I use it often, but words on paper require something more of us—a deeper effort, perhaps a sense of deeper caring. Just the act of picking up a pen, a sheet of paper, and an envelope and then sitting down to record on paper my thoughts, a prayer, a word of encouragement, or simply, 'I'm thinking of you.'

"Yes, it takes more time and effort than e-mail," June said, "but for me, the act of holding your letter in my hand, the letter you held in your hand and then put your words on that paper, made me feel closer, more 'in touch.'"

> *"Keeping in touch via words on paper links hearts and minds more personally than e-mail."*

Thank you, dear June, for that eloquent reminder. Taking the time to stay in touch with absent girlfriends by mail is an important way to nurture our friendships and keep that treasured girl connection to one another fresh and alive.

> More than kisses, letters mingle souls; for thus friends absent speak.
>
> *John Donne*

Girl Pearls Set aside some time to write your faraway friend. I know hardly anyone writes letters anymore—we're all too busy and it's time consuming, plus you have to go buy stamps, blah, blah, blah—but a few lines scrawled on a pretty card will mean the world to her. Think about it. Don't you love receiving special cards in the mail? Good friends are worth the trouble. (However, I'm not trying to guilt trip you here. If writing by snail mail is one more stressful thing to add to your way-too-long to-do list, then don't. Send an e-mail instead. It's short, sweet, and a relatively painless way to keep in touch.)

14

Kindred Spirits
and Dream Weavers

Meeting a new friend with whom you share
an instant rapport. That feeling of "You, too?
I thought I was the only one," as C. S. Lewis
says. These are the friendships
that give our spirits wings.

A friend is a second self.

Latin Proverb

Remember how the irrepressible Anne of Green Gables was always on the lookout for kindred spirits, or as she called them, "bosom friends"?

We all long for that and are blessed when we find this rare gift.

My writing pal Jan and her best friend Jeanne are the ultimate kindred spirits.

"Nobody wants us on the same team for games because we finish each others' sentences," said Jan. "People always ask us if we're sisters. We don't think we look alike, but it always happens. And whenever someone from the old singles group runs into one of us, they think we're the other.

"We think I was put up for adoption because there were too many kids in her family," Jan said with a laugh. "As an only child who's never seen a picture of my pregnant mother, I'm suspicious. It's too uncanny. We laugh about it all the time."

Jan and Jeanne are "the Pointless Sisters," crowned so in 1988 at a '50s party when they sang a song parody. "We've made fools of ourselves at showers, birthday parties, anniversary parties, even a wedding reception—upon request," said Jan. "We can do the Shirelles like nobody's business, and we love the Beach Boys: 'She'll have fun, fun, fun 'til her hubby

178

takes the Visa away . . .' We both have an off-key singing voice and lots of moxie."

The two friends also share the same clothing size and the same perfume, Elizabeth Taylor's White Diamonds.

"We'll go shopping separately and come home with the same outfit," Jan said. "We often give each other the same Christmas present. This year we both received 'Elvis: 30 Years of Hits.' We cracked up. So typical."

"Aside from the fact that she's redheaded, we could both be cut from the same Hobbit cloth—however, we are taller than most people from the Shire."

My friend Kim felt that kindred connection when she met Janet at a singles lunch one day.

"We clicked right away," Kim said. "We both finished other people's sentences with oddball statements. We're both short—I believe I have an inch on her—and aside from the fact that she's redheaded, we could both be cut from the same Hobbit cloth—however, we are taller than most people from the Shire."

When my best friend Lana and I met at a Bible study years ago, we had an instant single woman kindred spirit connection, having both suffered through recent broken relationships and now wanting to have the kind of relationship God wanted us to have, with our focus on him first.

Of course, it also helped that we loved to shop for bargains at thrift stores and flea markets, go to chick flicks where we consumed plenty of popcorn and chocolate, keep up with the latest Hollywood gossip through *People* magazine, have fun decorating the different places we lived together, AND eat great big bowls of ice cream and act silly.

My friend Pat and I share a kindred love of reading, decorating, and all things English, having been based in England during the same time period. We'll swap books all the time, and she's forever e-mailing me, "Do you have anything *good* to read?"

But I have to confess that Pat's a little more highbrow than me. She prefers pedigreed books—the classics, excellent nonfiction and biographies, or literary fiction.

And while I too adore beautiful literary fiction, biographies, and classics, I don't share Pat's love of politics or history. And my favorite not-so-guilty pleasure is a good mystery, usually of the English variety: Agatha Christie, P. D. James, Elizabeth George, or Anne Perry—although I also appreciate the American "alphabet" mystery series by Sue Grafton and the culinary mysteries of Diane Mott Davidson.

Happily, my English friend—another Pat—is also a mystery lover, so we share that special paperback connection.

I'm grateful for the kindred-spirit friends God has placed in my path.

And I've learned that he brings me bosom friends for different areas and times of my life—which wasn't always an easy thing to grasp.

When my lifelong dream of becoming a published author came true—at the age of forty—some of my oldest and dearest friends, who didn't share that writing kinship

I'm grateful for the kindred-spirit friends God has placed in my path.

connection with me, didn't "get" it. Yes, they were happy for me and pleased by my achievement, but they weren't bouncing off the walls with excitement. I'd call them, bubbling over with enthusiasm over my latest publishing news, and they'd murmur the appropriate polite response but weren't interested in every little detail.

And my feelings got hurt.

I couldn't understand why they weren't more thrilled for me. This was a really big deal to me—one of the most important things that had ever happened in my entire life.

Strange clerks in department stores were more enthusiastic than my friends were—"You wrote a BOOK?"

So to get the excited response I yearned for, I quickly learned to call my poet friend Katie—the queen of bouncing off the walls with excitement who wanted to hear every single comma and exclamation point of my new writing life—instead.

This was also the time in my life when my mom and I grew closer, because she, more than anyone else, had been there from the start when my writing dreams began.

Mom was there when I read 103 books in the first grade and declared, "I'm going to be a writer someday." She was there when I became the editor of my high school paper and had romantic visions of going overseas to become a foreign correspondent. She was also there when, upon graduating, I marched down to the major daily newspaper in town and announced that I wanted to be a reporter. And when the editor gently told me I needed a college degree or a little life experience first, my mom, understanding my inbred impatience, supported my enlisting in the Air Force instead.

Mom was also there when my enlistment ended and I went back to college—several times. And she was there many years later when I finally got my journalism degree.

So no one was more proud and excited for me than Mom when I received news of my first book contract. She told everyone she knew, "My daughter's an author!" and couldn't wait to hear every little publishing detail.

I couldn't understand why my close friends weren't equally excited.

Perhaps the fact that they weren't my mom had something to do with it.

Intellectually, I realized that it wasn't "their thing," and since I didn't want to bore them, I soon learned to keep my writing news to a minimum, sharing it instead with other writers who understood.

But it still hurt my heart.

Thankfully, in time God graciously brought me kindred-spirit writing girlfriends who, like me, are word lovers and understand when I call them up all excited to say, "Listen to this—isn't that just a perfect phrase? Don't you love it?"

These friends also share that neurotic writer thing.

Yes, I know it comes as a big surprise, but most writers are insecure and neurotic—especially when they're in the midst of creating a new work. (Read Anne Lamott's *Bird by Bird* for a great example.) It's simply part and paragraph of the trade. My writing pals "get it" when I whine, "What ever made me THINK I could write? This is a piece of garbage—the worst thing I've ever done. I hate it. It's trite and insipid. Now they're finally going to find out the truth and ask for their advance back. Blah, blah, blah . . ."

I love that writing kinship my pen girlfriends and I share and would be lost without it.

But I also love my bosom friends who aren't writers.

It wasn't until many years later when my poet friend Katie became an instant mom and I was pleased and happy for her but didn't understand her, what seemed to me, obsession with talking about the baby all the time that it finally dawned on me—*That's how my nonwriting friends must have felt when I talked about my new writing career all the time.* To them, it was just so much blah blah blah, the way babies, sports, or politics were to me.

Now I get it. My girlfriends don't have to share all my interests and dreams to love me and be true bosom friends.

And yet when I meet those kindred spirits who connect with my deepest dreams and truly understand my heart of hearts, they give my spirit wings.

Are we not like two volumes of one book?

Marceline Desbordes-Valmore

Girl Pearls Do something kindred with your bosom friend. For instance, if, like me, you're an avid reader, why not spend an evening browsing through one of those big megabookstores together? (The ones that have a little indoor café or coffee bar.) Then, once you've found your treasures, spend a leisurely hour or two sipping coffee or tea and chatting away about your favorite books. Or maybe you're in a shopping mood instead but don't want to spend a lot of money. It's always fun to get up early on a Saturday morning and go garage saleing with a girlfriend to find bargains.

15

Girlfriend Getaways

Sometimes you need more than Calgon to take
you away from it all—you need a girlfriend!

A good holiday is one spent among people whose notions
of time are vaguer than yours.

J. B. Priestley

on't be surprised if we find a dead critter or two inside," Jan warned me as she pushed open the door of her little cabin in the woods.

"A dead critter?!" I froze in my tracks.

"A mouse or a lizard . . ."

"A mouse or a lizard?! But how do they get *in* if the door's locked?" I asked in my clueless city-girl-scared-to-death-of-rodents-and-reptiles quaver.

"Through little holes . . ."

I hung back as Jan first scoped out the interior. Then I bravely followed her in once she gave the all clear.

Jan is five-foot-two with naturally curly blond hair (she reminds me a bit of the little girl from Charlie Brown with the "naturally curly hair") and you'd never know it to look at her, but this woman is *strong*.

I watched in amazement as my 120-pound girlfriend hoisted a four-foot axe and clomped out into the snow to split kindling for our fire.

Grizzly Adams has nothing on Jan. Oh, and this was *after* she'd gotten up at 7 A.M. and started a slow-simmering dinner for us that morning.

But then, Jan's a country girl.

When she lived in the country years ago, she had to get up

186

and feed the goats by 6 A.M., then see to the pigs and chickens, and then go in and cook breakfast for her daughters before sending them off to school. This woman even used to make her own goat cheese.

I felt privileged and secure to be in such hale and hearty company.

Jan and I had a productive day writing and wound up the second day of our girlfriend getaway with her yummy pork roast dinner followed by a great old Susan Hayward tearjerker from the '50s. It was a nice, lazy evening, and we were winding down to go to bed, when suddenly we heard voices outside our isolated cabin in the woods, then heavy feet running across the back deck (which was directly behind where I was sitting) and someone pounding on the door.

We both jumped off our respective couches in fright.

"Who is it? What do you want?" my trying-to-be-brave, yet trembling, country-girl friend Jan shouted, picking up the nearby axe.

"It's an emergency. There's a big ol' fire nearby," yelled a woman from outside the, what now looked to me to be paper thin, back door—which I now noticed, in growing terror, was unlocked.

"Jan," I hissed in a frightened whisper, "call the police or a neighbor!"

"The police would take twenty minutes to get here, and there are no neighbors around. We're the only ones out here."

And I thought I was scared before.

Next, I heard a man's voice mumbling something to the woman, and I became convinced they were going to break in and hurt us at any moment. (Not too far from where we were staying was where the three female Yosemite sightseers had been murdered a few years earlier. And the night before at dinner, Jan had mentioned they'd found the car and bodies "nearby.") Terrified, and with visions of being axe-murdered in my head, I cautiously inched over to the back door and quietly locked it.

Now we were safe—although I still harbored fears about them battering down the thin door to get to us.

"Okay, thank you," Jan yelled out to the unknown duo. "We'll call the fire department."

"Oh . . . Okay," and the two—at least we *think* it was two—strangers clomped off the deck together. Moments later, we heard a truck start up and spin down the snow-packed dirt road.

Jan, meanwhile, was furiously phoning the police and forest service to tell them what had happened. I waited a few minutes to make sure they were gone (for all I knew, one of them could have stayed behind, or there could have been a third person in the scary group) and peeked out the front window.

I've heard the phrase "pitch black" a thousand times, but

for the first time in my life I actually saw it. I couldn't see a thing. It was a scary, eerie feeling.

I started packing.

"We have to get out of here before they come back," I said to Jan, as she hung up the phone.

"I don't think they're going to come back," my country friend said reasonably.

"The Forest Service said they've got dozens of brush clean-up fires burning in the area—normal stuff they do every fall. No problem. They've had other calls. This couple was just trying to warn us."

"Maybe, maybe not," I replied in a shaky voice, "but I don't think I can stay here tonight. I didn't realize how vulnerable and isolated we were out here—and that there's no one close if we needed help, and—"

The phone rang, interrupting my hysterical outburst.

"They did? Oh, okay. Thanks," I heard Jan say.

"That was the sheriff's department," she said. "A couple that lives in the area just called in and told them they'd stopped by here to warn us about the fire, so it's nothing to worry about. They were just being good neighbors and watching out for us."

"Maybe," I said. "Or *maybe* they just called the sheriff's office to prevent them from coming out and checking on us—to throw them off the track. Once they know the coast is clear, they'll be back."

"Do you think maybe you read too many mysteries?" Jan said.

So much for our quiet girlfriends writing getaway.

I insisted that we throw a few things into a bag and drive into the nearest town to sleep in a nice, safe motel that night—my treat. And my kind, understanding, country-girl friend, knowing that I was scared out of my city-girl mind, graciously acquiesced.

For some reason, she hasn't invited me back to the cabin.

Jan's had more success on her girlfriend getaways with her best friend Jeanne.

Once a year the two friends head to the cute little cabin in the woods for their annual weeklong getaway and Scrabble marathon. Jeanne cooks gourmet meals while tomboy Jan splits the wood and takes care of the dead critters.

"We have incredible Bible studies and prayer time," Jan said. "We also take long hikes. Jeanne got me into hiking. I was never a hiker, but I just kept huffing and puffing until I got the stamina to keep up with her."

The friends also enjoy watching the outdoor movies under the stars at the nearby lake. "Even if the movie's stupid, we don't care," Jan said, "because we're going for the experience."

One year the two worked on a scrapbooking project to-

190

gether, reliving all their old trips. Another way they relive the trips is by reading the journal Jan keeps at the cabin.

Here's one sweet journal entry from Jeanne:

> Although ten days in England with Jan was "brilliant," there's nothing that can replace in my heart spending time at the cabin. It's a retreat, a refuge, a sanctuary. . . . Highlights include: our trip to Mono Lake and the tufa walk—with those beautiful mineral deposit sculptures rising from the saltwater lake—our picture album project, our outdoor Scrabble game at the Summit amidst splendid wildflowers, and, of course, our marathon of card and board games every evening. Thank you, Jan, my sister, my friend.

The women have also been on a few exotic getaways together.

In 1991 the two single best friends spent a month traveling through Europe by train—Germany, Switzerland, Austria, and Italy. "We did *Europe through the Back Door* à la Rick Steves," Jan said. "We used backpacks and put thirty days worth of clothes in them."

Then in 1994 the girlfriends traveled to Australia and New Zealand. The women went diving in the Great Barrier Reef, kicked around with some kangaroos, and got to cuddle a koala bear.

Fun times.

When I was stationed in England, my friend Diane and I went on some great girlfriend getaways together, too.

Like Paris.

We had a blast in the City of Lights—strolling along the Seine, climbing up the Eiffel Tower, drinking hot chocolate in a sidewalk café on the Champs d' Elysées, gazing in awe at the *Venus de Milo* in the Louvre, and meeting some cute guys at the USO.

We were young, single, and in Paris.

What can I say? We were young, single, and in Paris.

We had our pictures painted in Montmartre by struggling artists, ate delicious crepes from a creperie near the Arc de Triomphe, and danced in the famous Le Palace discothèque—this was the '70s, remember, and disco was hot.

Lana and I—who were single together during the first half of our thirties—haven't done anything quite as exciting, but we still had some fun girlfriend getaways.

We drove to Monterey and Carmel for a four-day weekend once, visiting the beautiful Monterey Bay Aquarium, walking along the boardwalk, and even eating at the famous Hog's Breath Inn in vain hopes of having restaurant owner Clint Eastwood make our day. No such luck.

Another time we went to San Clemente and stayed with Lana's cousin and visited the mega Calvary Chapel in Capistrano Beach.

Then there were the women's retreats with my church.

The large church I attended would offer once-a-year weekend retreats at a beautiful nearby hotel on a lake. It was fun, luxurious, and spiritual—and definitely not rustic—so Lana and I were both happy campers.

The two of us always had visions of New York or Europe, but our budgets never allowed for it. Someday . . .

My Aunt Sharon married into a family of eight brothers—real outdoorsy men who liked to go hunting each fall. So when the guys went hunting up north, the girls held their own special little getaway in southern Wisconsin.

"We hired a sitter for all the kids involved, had one house we all piled into, including sleeping bags, suitcases, dogs and cats," Sharon recalled. "We ordered a pizza, or had fun making one, and then we were off like Santa to the blue-light specials.

"No husband, no kids, no cooking. Wow. We were on our own. Look out Racine and Milwaukee. The girls were power shopping.

"With my sister-in-law's station wagon, off we went. Everyone heading to different departments—boys' toys, girls' toys —and then trying to fit everything into our vehicle. We all felt like Santa; we were only missing Rudolph to guide our wagon. We made it through snow-covered streets as we rode through downtown, laughing all the way. Then for supper, we headed to the Cozy Lounge and ordered our well-deserved petite filets."

My pal Jan's friend Mary Gail has been getting together with the same group of ten girlfriends for decades.

"Two of us met in kindergarten in 1949," said Mary Gail, "and out of the ten, seven of us married high school sweethearts. We were all in each other's weddings, and we have a lot of history together."

> *My pal Jan's friend Mary Gail has been getting together with the same group of ten girlfriends for decades.*

The girls first met in high school in southern California, where once a month they'd rotate houses for a slumber party. After they got married, they all still got together once a month at someone's house for lunch, and then, once the kids were born, they got together once a month in the park.

Eventually, however, the responsibilities of families, careers, moves, and other major life events interrupted the regular girlfriend get-togethers for a few seasons.

But about fifteen years ago, Sheila, one of the friends who had a house in Palm Springs, invited all the others over for a "girlfriend reunion." The women had so much fun together that they pledged then and there to make it a yearly tradition. In time, the house became a condo in Palm Desert, and now every April the ten women meet there for a five-day getaway.

Mostly, the women lay by the pool and visit, but they'll also read and play '50s songs from high school and often get up and dance.

"We act the same as when we were in high school," Mary Gail said with a laugh. "We relax and take turns fixing dinner. Most of the time we like to cook in, but we usually go out to dinner one night. We do a lot of talking. We've been through a lot over the years—divorces and things with our kids—and we're all a wonderful support group for each other. We're like the Ya-Ya Sisterhood—we've just really, really been there for one another. We've all made other friends along the way, but there's just something real special we have together."

That was evidenced last year when Mary Gail had heart surgery and Pam, her girlfriend since kindergarten, flew up to be with her and take care of her.

"She wouldn't take no for an answer," Mary Gail said.

The other friends have all done the same—in different ways—for each other at one time or another.

Nine of the women still live in California, but when Melinda, their Oregon friend, suddenly lost her fifty-six-year-old high school sweetheart husband to a heart attack a couple years ago, the girlfriends visited her in Oregon that year. "Our trip to see her was the most emotional yet," Mary Gail said.

The ten are now talking about taking a short cruise together the year they turn sixty—which is right around the corner.

"We're extremely close," said Mary Gail. "And as we get

older, we get more emotional about it, because some of us have health problems and we don't know how much more time we'll all have. We feel like we're closer today than ever. When you get to be this age, you realize life is short."

No matter what the age, girlfriend getaways are an important bonding ritual.

Heather, my Michigan colleague, says she enjoys spontaneous weekend getaways with her girlfriends, visiting Chicago and eating Cheesecake Factory cheesecake for breakfast while watching *Golden Girls* reruns. "It's the best!"

> *The ten are now talking about taking a short cruise together the year they turn sixty—which is right around the corner.*

Heather also once took a cross-country road trip to Colorado—sleeping in the van at truck stops on the way—with one of her girlfriends. "We went hiking in the mountains, but we were totally unprepared and ended up having to hike down the Rocky Mountains for three hours in the dark without a flashlight," she recalled, "but man, did we see an amazing sunset from the top."

On another road trip Heather reunited with some friends from high school for the first time in five years, and the four of them traveled from Michigan to Louisville, Kentucky.

"In the spirit of sisterhood, we all had something pierced—

196

eyebrow, belly button, tongue," she recalled. "And on the drive home, we bonded through our freshly pierced pain. Every once in a while, someone would bump a piercing and shriek in pain. It was the most hysterical drive home—and the most torturous.

"Of course, we eased our pain by stopping at every outlet mall between Kentucky and home."

When I first heard Heather's piercing remembrance, my middle-aged self was a little taken aback—the only thing I've ever had pierced was my ears, just one hole for one earring on each side. And I felt really old and couldn't relate.

But then a memory from nearly twenty-five years ago came back to me.

I, too, was in my early twenties but stationed in England at the time. One day, my Air Force roommate and I—in the spirit of sisterhood—decided to get tattoos. If memory serves me correctly (but it often doesn't, so don't quote me), she got a sweet little woodland scene of a butterfly flying over a mushroom on her hip.

I wanted Jonathan Livingston Seagull—this was the '70s, remember—but the artist didn't have a picture of this free-spirited bird in his tattoo repertoire. Lots of Harley David-sons, military insignias, hearts that said "Mom" (or any other woman's name), snakes, dragons, roses, daisies, and butterflies, but no Jonathan. So he'd have to draw it freehand.

Now, I've never been big on pain, so the idea of a guy

sketching freehand with a NEEDLE on my body wasn't terribly appealing. I quickly looked through the existing pictures in his tattoo portfolio—easily bypassing all the biker paraphernalia, skulls, snakes, and lizards—and finally settled on a sweet, delicate object often found in nature (a tiny piece of fruit), less than an inch in circumference—therefore, appropriately subtle and discreet.

I've always believed less is more.

And if we ever get together in a girlfriends-only getaway, I'll show it to you.

> Wishing to be friends is quick work, but friendship is a slow-ripening fruit.
>
> *Aristotle*

Girl Pearls Schedule a girlfriends getaway. What are you in the mood for? Some quiet and reflective spiritual time? Attend a weekend retreat together. Outdoor fun and games? Get together a group of your like-minded girlfriends and go skiing (as long as there's a great lodge with a roaring fire and plenty of chocolate) or camping. Or perhaps some much-needed pampering? Save up your money and indulge yourself by going on a spa getaway with your best friend—complete with facial, massage, and whatever else they do there. (This is one I still have yet to do myself. Are you listening, Lana?)

16

Girl Time

From book clubs to sewing circles and
everything in between—ideas for fun ways
to spend time with the girls.

The loneliest woman in the world is a woman
without a close woman friend.

George Santayana

Are you ready for a little girl time now?

Go for it! Don't wait—pick up the phone right now and call a girlfriend to invite her out to lunch, dinner, or a great chick flick you've both been wanting to see.

Not in the mood for food or a movie? Go shopping or to the gym instead.

The important thing is to spend *time* with your girlfriends. You need that girl connection—that sharing, that talking, that understanding—that only your women friends can provide.

And the man in your life will thank you for it, too.

Michael's always relieved when I have girl time with my friends, because then he knows I'm getting that chatting, communicating, and sympathetic-ear need taken care of by my girlfriends rather than him. Like most men, if I come to him with a problem, his logical mind wants to fix it—unless I forewarn him, "I just need you to listen to my troubles, not give me a solution." My girlfriends give me the tea and sympathy I crave.

Perhaps you're a little shy, or new in town and don't know too many women? Join a women's group. What are your interests?

200

Reading? Join—or start—a book club and finally read all those classics you've always been meaning to. Or pick the current best-sellers instead. It's up to you and your group.

Sports and Leisure? (a Trivial Pursuit category, by the way.) Join a local softball league; golf, tennis, or biking club; hiking group; bowling league. . . .

Sewing and needlework? Find a quilting, knitting, or sewing group to join. (But please excuse me if I don't participate. I'm needle impaired.)

Art? Take an art class at your local community college, volunteer to be a docent at an art museum in the area, or spend an evening going from one art gallery to another.

Crafts? There are a zillion and one crafts—from candle making to rubber stamping and scrapbooking—to choose from. Pick the one you prefer and connect with a group of crafty women once a month to create your favorite craft.

Check out your local paper, library, or church bulletin board to find groups with like interests. And if that doesn't work, surf the Net.

Whether you have one friend or ten, it's always fun to get together for dinner on a regular basis—or take turns making dinner for each other. That way you get your much-needed girl time *and* food. But if you'd prefer to expand your mind rather than your waistline, perhaps you'd like to take an English literature class together—or whatever interest you've always wanted to pursue (maybe seventeenth-century mapmaking?).

Another fun activity is to window shop together at a home improvement store—no men allowed—and fantasize about that dream kitchen or bathroom you've always wanted.

Whatever you do, allow yourself plenty of time together to talk and share, because that's what it's all about, girlfriend.

Or go out to a karaoke place with a group of girls and have fun pretending to be the Supremes or the Dixie Chicks.

There's no limit to the fun, memory-making girl-time things you can do.

But whatever you do, allow yourself plenty of time together to talk and share, because that's what it's all about, girlfriend.

Here I'd like to share something rather personal with you. The week before I finished writing this book, I had a little scare. When I went in for my annual checkup with my oncologist (I've been cancer free for more than ten years), he found a lump in my remaining breast.

I was terrified.

202

Even more so than when I was diagnosed with breast cancer more than a decade ago, because then I was clueless and figured it was nothing to worry about.

Now I know better. Also, there was that fear that everyone who's had cancer has: "What if it comes back? This time it could be fatal."

And Michael, who's usually very kind and sensitive (which I bragged about in *Thanks for the Mammogram!*), went into his male shut-down-the-emotions mode to cope—his self-defense mechanism to hide the terror that was flooding his whole body—which to me came across as cold and unfeeling.

I needed a girlfriend's understanding ear, but both my mom and Lana were unavailable. So I called my dear friend Pat, whom I've known for more than twenty-five years and who at different times in my life has been like a surrogate mom to me. Even though she was already in her white flannel pajamas—it was nearly 9:00 P.M. on a weeknight—she told me to come right over.

When I arrived, she greeted me at the door with a loving hug and a cup of tea. And she spent the next hour listening to me, asking the right questions, and offering encouraging words and prayers.

When I left, I felt much better. Her girl time was exactly what I needed. I had a mammogram and ultrasound a few days later, and they both came back normal. Thank you, Lord!

The first person I called was Michael.

The second was a girlfriend.

Stay is a charming word in a friend's vocabulary.

Louisa May Alcott

Acknowledgments

Gobs of girl-time gratitude to all of my girlfriends for the loving impact you've had on my life. You add laughter and music to my days and light and color to those occasional dark nights. I treasure you and our friendships.

Special thanks to:

Annette Smith, my sweet, southern-fried writing friend, for graciously reading several chapters when I was under the deadline gun and giving me your genteel but funny feedback. Now you go eat your greens, girl!

Katie Young, for allowing me to tell the Diaper Change story and for remaining my close friend even when I was a little self-absorbed and clueless.

Jan Coleman, my local writing pal, for correcting my neurotic remembrance of that infamous writing getaway in the woods and for always being willing—and flying-fingers fast—to give me fun anecdotes for my books. Jan, I appreciate you more than words can say.

Diane Melick, for that happy stroll down roommate memory lane. We'll always have Paris!

Dawn Alexander, for refreshing my high school memories.

June Varnum, my sweet pen friend, who came through at the last minute when I needed stories for that chapter.

Rene Gutteridge, for reminding me again what Braxton Hicks means.

My Aunt Sharon, for her fun hometown remembrances and our shared food connection. You're due for another visit!

Kari Jameson and Jennie (Jameson) Damron, my two nieces and surrogate "daughters," whom I love to pieces. Thanks for all the great stories, girls!

Sheri Jameson, for being so much more than a sister-in-law. I consider it a privilege to call you my friend. Your wise and godly example is one I strive to emulate. Thanks also for your love and understanding ear when I needed it the most.

Pat McLatchey, one of my oldest friends, who provided a much-needed shoulder during a scary time and who also took the time to share the wonderful details of her ladies tea group.

Lana Yarbrough, for being my best friend through thick and thin.

Lonnie Hull DuPont, my kindred-spirit editor and beloved

friend. Working with you is a privilege. Being your friend is an even greater one. Thanks for your gentle editorial guidance. Wish we didn't live so far apart so we could spend some more chick-flick and chatter time together.

Warm gratitude to my agent par excellence, Chip Macgregor. I think it's about time to make you an honorary "girlfriend," Chip. I appreciate you and all you do on my behalf. You're the best.

My mom and my sister Lisa, for always being there. And for being not just relatives, but friends. I love you.

And, as always, my deepest thanks to my Renaissance-man husband, Michael, for his continual love and support—and for cooking when I'm on deadline. Being married to you is better than Disneyland, honey! (Shut the door.)

Lastly, thanks to all the women who took the time to share girl-time nuggets from their lives: Dawn Alexander, Heather Brewer, Karen Campbell, Kathy Christensen, Jan Coleman, Debbie Cullifer, Jennie Damron, Lonnie Hull DuPont, Bettie Eichenberg, Bettie Fiscus, Karen Grant, Sharon Hetland, Marian Hitchings, Kari Jameson, Sheri Jameson, Mary Gail Maxwell, Pat McLatchey and her tea group, Diane Melick, Jamie Miller, Joanne Mordja, Marya Morgan, Kim Orendor, Joyce Pope, Leona Reinhardt, Annette Smith, Cathleen Snyder, Toni Terrell, Ingrid Van Dyck, June Varnum, Denise Williams, and Katie Young.

Laura Jensen Walker is the author of several humor books, including *Dated Jekyll, Married Hyde; Love Handles for the Romantically Impaired; Thanks for the Mammogram!; Mentalpause;* and *Through the Rocky Road and Into the Rainbow Sherbet.* A popular speaker and breast cancer survivor, she knows firsthand the healing power of laughter. She and her husband, Michael, live in Sacramento, California.

For information on having Laura Jensen Walker speak at your event, please contact Speak Up Speaker Services toll free at (888) 870-7719 or e-mail Speakupinc@aol.com. To learn more about Laura, please visit her web site at www.laurajensenwalker.com. To write Laura, please e-mail her at Ljenwalk@aol.com or write to her at P.O. Box 601325, Sacramento, CA 95860.